Easy Spanish for Construction
Inglés Fácil para Construcción

Two-way Translation Guide for
Construction, Lawn & General Use

Easy to Say

Many Useful Words and Phrases

Guía de Traducción en dos Idiomas
para la Construcción, Césped y Uso
General

Fácil de Decir

Muchas Palabras y Frases Útiles

COMMUNICATION	COMUNICACIóN
LANGUAGES	IDIOMAS
LEARNING	APRENDIZAJE
TEAMWORK	COOPERACIóN
SAFETY	SEGURIDAD

CONTENTS

CONTENIDO

DAILY PHRASES	FRASES DIARIAS

Good morning!	**(Frase en Inglés)**
gud MORning!	(pronunciación)
¡Buenos Días!	**(Spanish phrase)**
¡BWAYnos DEFus!	(pronunciation)
How are you?	**Good, and you?**
jau AR iu?	gud, and iu?
¿Cómo estás?	**Bien, Y tú?**
¿COmo essTAHS?	bee-in, ee too?
Excuse me...	**I'm...**
eksKIUS mi...	aim...
Perdón...	**Soy...**
pairDOAN...	soy...
Can you help me?	**Thank you.**
can iu jelp mi?	zank iu.
¿Puede ayúdame?	**Gracias.**
¿PWEHdeh aYOOdarmay?	GRAHsyus.
Please...	**You're welcome.**
pliis...	iour UELcom.
Por favor...	**De nada.**
por faVOR...	deh NAda.

Yes	**No.**	**Maybe.**
ies.	nou.	meibi
Sí.	**No.**	**Quizá**
see.	no.	kee-SA

Hello, Sir!
jeLOU, sur!
¡Hola, Señor!
¡OHla, senYOR!

What's your name, please?
juats ior NEIM, pliis ?
¿Cómo te llamas, por favor?
¿COmo tay YAmas, por faVOR?

My name is...
mai neim is...
Mi nombre es...
me NOhmbray ess...

Nice to meet you.
nais tu MIIT iu.
Mucho gusto.
MOOcho GOOsto.

What is your phone number?
juat is ior foun NOMber?
¿Cuál es su número de teléfono?
¿kwall ess soo NOOmero day teLAYfono?

What is the address?
juat is de aDRES?
¿Cuál es la dirección?
¿kwall ess la deerekSYOHN?

DIRECTIONS

DIRECCIONES

Where is it?
juer is it?
¿Dónde está?
¿DOANday esTA?

Here is the address.
jir is de aDRES.
Aquí está la dirección.
aKEE esTA la deerckSYOHN.

Let's go, please.
lets gou, pliis.
Vámonos, por favor.
VAmohnohs, por faVOR.

Follow me / the map.
FAlou mi / de map.
Síga me / el mapa.
SEEga may / el MApa.

D0311633

Go straight / left / right.
gou streit / left / rait.
Vaya a la delante / izquierda / derecha.
VAya ah la deLAHNtay / eesKYAIRda / deREHcha.

Meet me there -- at six o'clock.
miit mi der -- at siks ouCLOK.
Encuéntreme allí -- a las seis en punto.
enKWENtramay aYEE -- ah las sayss en POONtoh.

OCCUPATIONS ## OCUPACIONES

Are you a painter?
ar iu a PEINter?
¿Es usted un pintor?
¿es ooSTED oon peenTOR?

I need a carpenter.
ai niid a CARpenter.
Necesito un carpintero.
neceSEEtoh oon carpeenTEHro.

contractor CONtracter	**contratista** cohntraTEEsta
electrician elecTRIchian	**electricista** electreeSEEsta
gardener GARDner	**jardinero** hardeeNAYro
landscaper LANDskeiper	**paisajero** paisaHAIRo
mason MEIson	**albañil** allbahnYEEL
plasterer PLASterer	**yesero** yehSAIRo
plumber PLOmer	**plomero** ploMAYro
repairman riPERman	**reparador** rehparaDOR
roofer RUUfer	**techero** tehCHAIRo
truck driver troc DRAIver	**camionero** cahmyoNAYro
worker UERker	**trabajador** trabahaDOR

Fill this out, please.
fil dis aut, pliis.
Complete esto, por favor.
cohmPLEHtay ESStoh, por faVOR.

Do you have tools / a card?
du iu jav tuuls / a card?
¿Tiene su las herramientas / una tarjeta?
¿TYEHneh lahs airaMYENtahs / oona tarHEHta?

6

COMMUNICATION COMUNICACIÓN

How do you say...?
jau du iu sei...?
¿Cómo se dice...?
¿COmo say DEEsay...?

What's this called?
juats dis cold?
¿Cómo se llama esto?
¿COmo say YAma EStoh?

Do you speak English / Spanish?
du iu spiik INglich / SPANich?
¿Hablas Inglés / Español?
¿AHblas eenGLACE / esspahnYOHL?

I speak a little.
ai spiik a LItl.
Hablo un poco.
AHblo oon POco.

Please repeat slowly.
pliis ripiit SLOUli.
Repita, despacio, por favor.
rehPEEta, dehSPAsyo, por FAHvor.

Can someone interpret?
can SOMuon inTERpret?
¿Puede alguien interpretar?
¿PWEHdeh ALLgyen eentairprehTAR?

COMMUNICATION   COMUNICACIÓN

What does this mean?
juat dos dis miin?
¿Que quiere decir esto?.
¿kay KYAYreh deSEER EStoh?

What is this?
juat is dis?
¿Qué es esto?
¿kay ess ESStoh?

It doesn't matter..
it DOsent MATer
No importa.
no eemPORtah.

What?	**Write it.**
juat?	rait it.
¿Qué?	**Escríbalo.**
¿kay?	esCREEbalo.
Do you know how?	**Tell him.**
du iu nou jau?	tel jim.
¿Sabe cómo?	**Dígale.**
¿SAHbeh COmo?	DEEgalay.
Understand?	**I don't understand.**
onderSTAND?	ai dount onderSTAND.
¿Entiende?	**Yo no entiende.**
¿enTYENday?	yo no enTYENday.

QUESTIONS AND REPLIES
PREGUNTAS Y RESPUESTAS

What? juat?	**¿Qué**? kay?
What time? juat taim?	**¿Qué hora**? kay OHra?
Which? juich?	**¿Cuál**? kwall?
How? jau?	**¿Cómo**? COmo?
How many? jau MEni?	**¿Cuántos**? KWANtohs?
How much? jau moch?	**¿Cuánto**? KWANtoh?
Where? juer?	**¿Dónde**? DOANday?
When? juen?	**¿Cuándo**? KWANdoh?
Why? juai?	**¿Por qué**? por kay?
Why not? juai not?	**¿Cómo no**? COmo no?
Who? ju?	**¿Quién**? kyen?
This dis	**Esto** EStoh
That dat	**Eso** ESo
These diis	**Estos** EStohs
Those dous	**Esos** ESohs
a little a LItl	**Poquito** poKEEtoh
a lot a lot	**Muchos** MOOchohs
Less les	**Menos** MEHnohs
More mor	**Mas** mahs
Here jier	**Aquí** ahKEE
There der	**Allí** ahYEE
Now nau	**Ahora** ahOHra
Later LEIter	**Más tarde** mas TARday
I ai	**Yo** yo
Me mi	**Yo** yo
You iu	**Usted** ooSTED
Him jim	**El** el
Them dem	**Los** lohs

9

TEAMWORK | ## COOPERACIÓN

Help me.
JELP mi.
Ayúdame.
ahYOOdamay.

Help him.
JELP jim.
Ayúdalo.
ahYOOdalo.

Like this.
laik dis.
Así.
ahSEE.

Not like that.
not laik dat.
Así no.
ahSEE no.

Show me.
chou mi.
Muéstreme.
MWEStraymay.

Good.
gud.
Bien.
BEE-en.

Continue...
conTINiu...
Siga...
SEEga...

Stop.
stop.
Pare.
PAreh.

Wait.
ueit.
Espere.
essPEHreh.

I want...
ai uant...
Quiero...
KYEHro...

What do you need?
juat du iu niid?
¿Qué necesita?
¿kay neceSEEtahs?

Point to it.
point tu it.
Indíquelo.
eenDEEkeilo.

SAFETY	SEGURIDAD
Use / Wear...	**a hard hat.**
ius / uer...	a jard jat.
Usa...	**un casco.**
OOsa...	oon CAHSco.

boots buuts	**botas** BOtas
ear plugs iar plogs	**tapones** taPOnehs
gloves glovs	**los guantes** GWANtes
goggles GOgels	**los anteojos** antiOhohs
harness JARnes	**arnés** arNESS
helmet JELmet	**un casco** oon CAHSco
mask mask	**máscara** MAHScara
respirator RESpireitor	**respirador** rehspeeraDOR
face shield feis chiild	**escudo de cara**
	esCOOdoh deh CAra

protection for ears / eyes
proTECchon for irs / ais.
protección para oídos / ojos.
protecseeOWN PAra ohEEdohs / OHhohs.

It is safe / not safe.
it is seif / not seif.
Está seguro / no está seguro.
esTA seGOOro / no esTA seGOOro.

Tell me if you get hurt.
tell mi if iu get jurt.
Dígame si se lastima.
DEEgamay see say lasTEEma.

Call 911.
coll nain-uan-uan.
Llame nueve-uno-uno.
YAmay NWAYvay-OOno-OOno.

I'm sick / injured.
aim sik / INllurd.
Estoy enfermo / lesionado.
esTOY enFAIRmo / lehsyoNAdoh.

Go home / to the clinic.
gou joum / tu de CLInic.
Vaya a su casa / a la clínica.
VAya ah soo CAsa / ah la KLEEneeka.

First aid.
furst eid.
Primeros auxilios.
preeMAIRohs ah ookSEALyohs.

bandage BANdch	**vendage** VENdaheh
Careful! KEIRful!	**¡Cuidado!** kweeDAdoh!
Clinic cli-nic	**clínica** KLEEneeka
doctor DOCtor	**doctor** docTOR
Help! jelp!	**¡Socorro!** ¡soCORo!
Help me. jelp mi.	**Ayúdame** aYOOdamay.
hospital jospital	**hospital** ohspeeTAL
Hurt? jurt?	**¿Herido?** airEEdoh?
Sick? sik?	**¿Enfermo?** enFAIRmo?

DAYS

today tuDEI
tomorrow tuMOrou
yesterday IESterdei
Monday MONdei
Tuesday TUSdei
Wednesday UENSdei
Thursday ZURSdei
Friday FRAIdei
Saturday SAturdei
Sunday SONdei

DÍAS

hoy día oy DEEya
mañana mahnYAna
ayer ahYAIR
Lunes LOOnes
Martes MARtes
Miercoles MYAIRkoles
Jueves HWAYves
Viernes VYAIRnes
Sábado SAbadoh
Domingo dohMEENgo

COLORS

light lait
dark dark
beige beich
black blak
blue blu
brown braun
clear kliir
gold GOULd
gray grei
green griin
orange ORench
pink pink
purple PURpul
red red
silver SILver
tan tan
white juait
yellow IELou

COLORES

claro CLAro
oscuro ohSCOOro
crema CRAYmah
negro NAYgro
azul ahSOOL
café cahFAY
claro CLARo
dorado dohRAdoh
gris greess
verde VAIRday
anaranjado anaRAHhadoh
rosa ROsa
morado moRAHdoh
rojo ROho
plata PLAta
crema CREHma
blanco BLAHNco
amarillo amaREELyo

ACTION!	¡ACCIÓN!
Carry it.	**Dig** here.
KEIRi it.	dig jir.
Lléva lo.	**Excava** aquí.
YEHva lo.	exCAva aKEE.
Bend bend	**Dobla** DOHbla
Break breik	**Rompe** ROAMpeh
Bring bring	**Trae** TRAeh
Carry KEIRi	**Lleva** YEHva
Change cheinch	**Cambia** CAHMbeea
Check chek	**Revisa** reVEEsa
Clean cliin	**Limpia** LEEMpya
Close clous	**Cierra** SYAIRra
Cover COver	**Cubre** COObreh
Cut cot	**Corta** CORta
Dig dig	**Excava** eksCAva
Do du	**Haga** AHga
Empty EMti	**Vacia** vaSEEa
Fill fil	**Llena** YAYna
Find faind	**Busca** BOOska
Fix fiks	**Arregla** aRAYgla
Glue glu	**Pege** PAYgeh
Grab grab	**Agárra** aGARra
Hang jang	**Cuelgue** KWELgay
Help jelp	**Ayuda** aYOOda
Hit jit	**Golpée** golPEHeh
Hold jould	**Sostenge** soSTAINgeh
Lift lift	**Levante** layVAHNteh
Load loud	**Carga** CARga
Lower LOUer	**Baje** BAhay
Make meik	**Haga** AHga
Mix miks	**Mezcla** MESScla

ACTION!	**¡ACCIÓN!**
Move muv	**Mueve** MWAYveh
Open O-pen	**Abre** AHbreh
Paint peint	**Pinta** PEENta
Pick up pik op	**Recoge** rehCOheh
Pull puul	**Jala** HAla
Push puch	**Empuja** emPOOha
Remove riMUUV	**Quita** KEEta
Repair riPEIR	**Repara** rehPAra
Repeat riPIIT	**Repite** rehPEEteh
Return riTURN	**Devuelve** deVWELveh
Sand sand	**Lija** LEEha
Scrape screip	**Raspa** RAHSpa
Spread spred	**Esparsa** esPARsa
Stack stak	**Apila** ahPEEla
Start start	**Empieza** emPEEehsa
Stop stop	**Pare** PAreh
Take teik	**Toma** TOHma
Tie tai	**Amarre** aMARreh
Tighten TAIten	**Apriéte** ahpreeEhtay
Turn off turn off	**Apaga** aPAga
Turn on turn on	**Prende** PRENdeh
Unload onloud	**Descarga** DEHScarga
Use ius	**Usa** OOsa
Wash uach	**Lava** LAva
Watch uatch	**Mira** MEEra
Work uerk	**Trabaja** traBAha

Notes / Notas:

it = lo	Don't = No
Paint it = Pintalo	Don't paint it. = No pintalo.
Load it = Cargalo	Don't load it. = No cargalo.
etc.	etc.

NUMBERS

NÚMEROS

1/16"	uan SIKStiintz	**un diez y seis** oon dyess ee sayss
1/8"	uan eitz	**un octavo** oon ohkTAvo
3/16"	zri SIKStiints	**tres diez y seis** trehs dyess ee sayss
1/4"	uan CORter	**un cuarto** oon KWARtoh
3/8"	zri eitz	**tres octavos** trehs ohkTAvohs
1/2"	jaf	**medio** MEHDyo
5/8"	faiv eitz	**cinco octavos** SEENco oakTAvohs
3/4"	zri CORters	**tres cuartos** trehs KWARtohs
7/8"	SEven eitz	**siete octavos** SYEHtay oakTAvohs

0.	**zero** SIrou	**cero** SEHro
1.	**one** uan	**uno** OOno
2.	**two** tu	**dos** dohs
3.	**three** zri	**tres** trehs
4.	**four** for	**cuatro** KWAtro
5.	**five** faiv	**cinco** SEENco
6.	**six** siks	**seis** sayss
7.	**seven** SEven	**siete** SYEHtay
8.	**eight** eit	**ocho** OHcho
9.	**nine** nain	**nueve** NWAYveh
10.	**ten** ten	**diez** DEEes
11.	**eleven** iLEven	**once** OWNseh
12.	**twelve** tuelv	**doce** DOHseh

13. **thirteen** ZURtiin	**trece** TRAYseh	
14. **fourteen** FORtiin	**catorce** caTORseh	
15. **fifteen** FIFtiin	**quince** KEENseh	
16. **sixteen** SIKStiin	**diez y seis** Dyess ee sace	
17. **seventeen** SEventiin	**diez y siete** Dyess ee SYEHtey	
18. **eighteen** EITiin	**diez y ocho** Dyess ee OHcho	
19. **nineteen** NAINtiin	**diez y nueve** Dyess ee NWAYveh	
20. **twenty** TUENti	**veinte** VAINteh	
21. **twentyone** TUENti-uan	**veintiuno** vainteeOOno	
22. **twentytwo** TUENti-tu	**veintidós** vainteeDOHS	
30. **thirty** ZURti	**treinta** TRAINta	
40. **forty** FORti	**cuarenta** kwaRENta	
50. **fifty** FIFti	**cincuenta** seenKWENta	
60. **sixty** SIKSti	**sesenta** sehSENta	
70. **seventy** SEventi	**setenta** sehTENta	
80. **eighty** EIti	**ochenta** ohCHENta	
90. **ninety** NAINti	**noventa** noVENta	
100. **one hundred** uan JONdred	**cien** syen	
1st. **first** furst	**primero** preMEHro	
2nd. **second** SEcond	**segundo** sehGOONdoh	
3rd. **third** zurd	**tercero** terSEHro	
---- **last** last	**último** OOLteemo	

SIZE

TAMAÑO

Make it this...
meik it dis...
Hágalo de este...
AHgalo day EStay...

size.
sais.
tamaño.
taMAHNyo.

long long
wide uaid
deep diip
high jai

largo LARgo
ancho AHNcho
hondo OWNdoh
alto ALLtoh

Make it	____ **feet**	____ **inches.**
meik it	____ fiit	____ INches.
Hágalo de	____ **pies**	____ **pulgadas.**
AHgalo day	____ Pyes	____ poolGAdas.

1x6 uan bai six

uno por seis
OOno por sayss

2x4 tu bai for

dos por cuatro
dohs por KWAtro

inch inch
foot fut
yard iard
Measure it. MEchur it.
gallon(s) GALon(s)
pound(s) paund(s)
shovelfull CHOvelful
square foot skueir fut

pulgada poolGAda
pie PEEeh
yarda YARda
Mídelo. MEEdelo.
galón(es) gaLOn(es)
libra(s) LEEbra(s)
palada paLAda
cuadrada pie
kwaDRAda PEEeh

square yard skueir iard

yarda cuadrada
HARda kwaDRAda

ADJUSTMENTS

AJUSTES

Make it...
meik it...
larger.
LARcher.
Hágalo más...
AHgalo mahs...
grande.
GRAHNde.

smaller SMOler	**pequeno** payKENyo
darker DARker	**oscuro** ohSKOOro
lighter LAITer	**claro** CLAro
larger LARcher	**grande** GRAHNday
longer LONGer	**largo** LARgo
shorter CHORter	**corto** CORtoh
looser LOOser	**suelto** SOOELtoh
tighter TAIter	**firme** FIRmeh

Move it....
muv it...
up.
op.
Muevalo...
MWAYvalo...
arriba.
aREEba.

a little a LItel	**un poco** oon POco
a lot a LOT	**mucho** MOOcho
back bak	**atrás** ahTRAHS
down daun	**abajo** aBAho
here jir	**aquí** ahKEE
there der	**allí** ahYEE
left left	**izquierda** eesKWAIRda
right rait	**derecha** dayRAYcha
less les	**menos** MEHnohs
more mor	**más** mahs
forward FORuard	**adelante** ahdeLAHNteh
Enough! iNOF	**¡Bastante!** ¡baSTAHNtay!

TIME

TIEMPO

What time is it?
juat taim is it?
¿Qué hora es?
¿kay OHra es?

At what time?
at juat taim?
¿A qué hora?
¿ah kay OHra?

1:00
It's one o'clock.
its uan o'CLOK.
Es la una.
es la OOna.

2:00
It's two o'clock.
its tu o'CLOK.
Son las dos.
sohn lahs dohs.

3:00
It's three o'clock.
its zri o'CLOK.
Son las tres.
sohn lahs trace.

4:15
At four fifteen.
at for fifTIIN.
A las cuatro quince.
ah lahs KWAtro KEENseh.

5:30
Five thirty.
faiv ZURti.
Cinco y treinta.
SEENco ee TRAINta.

6:45
Six forty five.
siks FORti faiv.
Seis y cuarenta cinco.
sayss ee kwaRENta SEENco.

Ten to seven.
ten tu SEven.
Siete menos diez.
SYEHtay MEHnohs DEEes.

Twenty past eight.
TUENti past eit.
Ocho y veinte.
OHcho ee VAINtay.

morning MORning
noon nuun
afternoon afterNUUN
night nait

mañana mahnYAna
mediodía medyoDEEa
tarde TARdeh
noche NOchay

MONEY	DINERO
How much?	**It costs...**
jau moch?	it cost...
¿Cuánto?	**Cuesta...**
KWANtoh?	KWESSta...

$10	**$10.25**
Ten dollars.	**Ten twenty five.**
ten DOLars.	ten tuenti-faiv.
Diez dólares.	**Diez veinti-cinco**
Dyess DOHlahress.	Dyess VEHNti-SEENco.

$10.50	**$10.75**
Ten fifty.	**Ten seventy five.**
ten FIFti.	ten SEventi-faiv.
Diez cincuenta.	**Diez setenta y cinco.**
Dyess seenKWENta.	Dyess sehTENta ee SEENco.

$100
One hundred dollars.
uan JONdred DOLars.
Cien dólares.
syen DOHlahress.

$236
Two hundred thirty six dollars.
tu JONdred ZURti siks DOLars.
Doscientos treinta seis dólares.
dohs-SYENtohs TRAINta sayss DOHlahress.

bank bank	**banco** BAHNco
bill bil	**billete** beYEtay
cents cents	**centavos** cenTAvohs

[Numbers / Números... page 16]

SCHEDULE/PAY   HORARIO/PAGA

Can you work   **from____ till____?**
can iu uerk   from____ til____?
¿Puede trabaja   **desde____ hasta___?**
¿PWEHdeh traBAja   desde____hasta___?

I can work...   **at six.**
ai can uerk...   at siks.
Puedo trabaja...   **a las seis.**
PWEHdoh traBAha...   ah lahs sayss.

I charge   **____ an hour.**
ai charch   ____ an AUer.
Yo cobro   **____ la hora.**
yo CObro   ____ la OHra.

I can pay   **____ dollars per hour.**
ai can pei   ____ DOlars per AUer.
Puedo paga   **____ dólares por hora.**
PWEHdoh PAga   ____ DOHlares por OHra.

I can pay you...   **today / Friday.**
ai can pei iu...   tuDEI / FRAIdei.
Puedo pagarlé...   **hoy / viernes**
PWEHdoh pagarLAY...   oy / VYAIRnes.

Pay me in cash   **with a check.**
pei mi in cach   uid a chek.
Pagueme en efectivo   **con cheque.**
pagWEHmeh en efecTEEvo   cohn CHEHkay.

SCHEDULE/PAY   HORARIO/PAGA

How late can you work?
jau leit can iu uerk?
¿Qué tan tarde puede trabajar?
¿kay tahn TARdeh PWEHdeh trabaHAR?

How early?
jau ERli?
¿Qué tan temprano?
¿kay tahn temPRAno?

Can you work tomorrow?
can iu uerk tuMOrou?
¿Puede trabajar mañana?
¿PWEHdeh trabaHAR mahnYAna?

Be here at...
bi jir at...
Este aquí a las...
ESteh ahKEE ah lahs...

See you tomorrow.
si iu tuMOrou.
Hasta mañana.
AHsta mahnYAna.

Break breik (rest)		**descanso** dehsCAHNso	
Date? deit?		**¿Fecha?** ¿FEHcha?	
Fill out fil aut		**Complete** comPLEHteh	
Lunch lonch		**Almuerzo** allMWAIRso	
Start at... start at...		**Empieza a las** emPYEHsa...	
Stop at... stop at...		**Pare a las..** PAreh ah lahs..	

LAWN CARE   CUIDO DE CÉSPED

Mow   the lawn.
mou   de loon.
Corta   el césped.
CORta   el SESped.

Fertilize fertilais   **Abona** aBOna
Rake reik   **Rastrilla** raSTREEya
Seed siid   **Siembra** seeEMbra
Water UAter   **Rega** REHga

Edge around   **the driveway.**
edch aRAUND   de DRAIVuei.
Corta alrededor   **del entrada.**
CORta allraydayDOR   del enTRAda.

garden GARden   **jardin** harDEEN
lawn loon   **césped** SESped
patio patio   **patio** PAtyo
planters PLANters   **macetas** maSAYtahs
trees triis   **árboles** ARbowles
trench trench   **la zanja** SANha
vines vains   **las vides** VEEDes
walkways UACueis   **las aceras** aSAYrahs
walls uaals   **los paredes** paREDes

Turn on the sprinklers   **For ___ minutes.**
turn on de SPRINklers   for ___ MInuts.
Abra las aspersores   **Por ___ minutos.**
AHbra las ahspairSOREs   por ___ meNOOtohs.

Lawn Care   Cuido de Césped

Use the blower.
ius de BLOUer.
Usa el soplador.
OOsa el soplaDOR.

Trim the bushes.
trim de BUCHes.
Poda los arbustos.
POda lohs arBOOstohs.

Turn over the soil.
turn OUver de soil.
Voltea la tierra.
volTAYa la TYAIRra.

Roll up the hose(s).
roul op de jous(es).
enrolla la manguera(s).
enROya la mahnGEHra(s).

Apply insecticide.
aPLAI inSECtisaid.
aplica insecticida.
ahPLEEca eensecteeSEEda.

Plant the flowers here / like this.
plant de FLAUers jir / laik dis.
Planta las flores aquí / así.
PLAHNta las FLORes ahKEE / ahSEE.

LAWN CARE CUIDO DE CÉSPED

Remove the weeds.
riMUUV de uiidz.
Saque los yerbajos.
SAkay lohs airBAhohs.

Clean out the leaves.
cliin aut de livs.
Saque las hojas.
SAkay lahs Ohahs.

Put them in bags / trashcans.
put dem in baks / TRACHcans.
Pon en bolsas / basureros.
pon en BOHLsahs / basooRAIRohs.

faucet FOset	**la llave** YAHveh
fruit frut	**la fruta** FROOta
hoe jou	**azadón** asaDOAN
nozzle NOsel	**boquilla** boKEEya
poison POIson	**veneno** vehNAYno
prune prun	**poda** POda
weeds uiidz	**yerbajos** jairBAhohs
gardener GARDner	**jardinero** hardeeNEHro
lawnmower LONmouer	**cortacésped** cortaSESped
mulch molch	**cubrir con paja** cooBREER cohn PAha
vegetables VECHtebol	**los vegetales** lohs vehehTALes

PAINTING   PINTAR

Paint...	the fence.
peint...	de fens.
Pinta...	**la cerca.**
PEENta...	la SAIRka.

ceiling SIILin	**el techo** TAYcho
door dor	**la puerta** PWAIRta
trim trim	**el borde** BORday
wall ual	**la pared** paRED

Use...	the brush.
ius...	de broch.
Usa...	**la brocha.**
OOsa...	la BROcha.

caulk cok	**calafate** calaFAtay
pan pan	**la cacerola** casayROla
roller ROLer	**el rodillo** roDEEyo
sprayer SPREIer	**rociadora** roseeaDORa

Cover it with...	**drop cloth**
COver it uiz...	drop cloz
Cúbralo con...	**el trapo**
COObralo cohn...	el TRApo

masking tape	**cinta enmasca**
MASking teip	SEENta enMASca

Ask for it.
ask for it.
Pídelo.
PEEdelo.

Attach the connectors.
aTACH de coNEKtors.
Ate los conectores.
AHteh lohs cohnecTORes.

Be careful with this.
bi KEIRful uiz dis.
Tenga cuidado con esto.
TENga kweeDAdoh cohn ESStoh.

Brace the wall.
breis de ual.
Arriosta la pared.
ahreeOHsta la paRED.

Bring me the paint / that board.
brin mi de peint / dat bord.
Traígame la pintua / esa tabla.
TRYgamay la peenTOOra / esa TAbla.

Build the wall here.
bild de ual jiir.
Construya la pared aquí.
cohnSTROOya la paRED ahKEE.

Handy Phrases

Frases Útiles

Call me.
col mi.
Llámame.
YAHmamay.

Call him.
col jim.
Llámalo.
YAHmalo.

Can I help you?
can ai jelp iu?
¿Puedo ayudale?
¿PWEHdoh aYOOdalay?

Can you help me?
can iu jelp mi?
¿Puede ayúdame?
¿PWEH-deh aYOOdamay?

Can you do this?
can iu du dis?
¿Puede hacer esto?
¿PWEHdeh ahSAIR EStoh?

Can you give me...?
can iu giv mi...?
Puedo darme...?
PWEHdoh DARmay...?

Carry it over here.
KEIRi it OUver jir.
Llevelo aquí.
YEHvelo ahKEE.

Caulk the cracks / joints.
kok de craks / choints.
Calafete las grietas / uniónes.
cahlaFEHteh lahs greeEHtas / ooneeOWNes.

Check the oil / breaker.
chek de oil / BREIker.
Revisa el aceite / cortacircuitos.
rehVEEsa el ahseEEteh / corta-seerKWEEtohs.

Change the blade / battery.
cheinch de bleid / BATeri.
Cambia la cuchilla / batería.
CAHMbeea la coCHEELya / batehREEya.

Clean the floors / windows.
cliin de flors / UINdous.
Limpia los pisos / estas ventanas.
leemPEEa lohs PEEsohs / EStahs venTAnas.

Clear the hall.
clir de jol.
Despeja el pasillo.
desPAYha el paSEEyo.

Close the windows when you leave.
clous de UINdous juen iu liiv.
Cierra las ventanas al irte.
SYAIRra lahs venTAnas ahl EERtay.

Handy Phrases

Come with me.
com uiz mi.
Venga conmigo.
VENga cohnMEgo.

Cover the floors.
COver de flors.
Cubre lohs pisos.
COObreh lohs PEEsohs.

Cut it here.
cot it jir.
Cortalo aquí.
CORtalo ahKEE.

Cut it at an angle... forty-five (45) degrees.
cot it at an EINgol... FORti faiv (45) deGRIIS.
Córtelo a un ángulo... de cuarenta y cinco grados.
CORtelo ah oon AHNgoolo...
                deh kwaRENta ee SEENco GRAHdohs.

Dig a hole / trench here.
dig a joul / trench jir.
Excava un hojo / zanja aquî.
exCAva oon OHho / SANha ahKEE.

Dig this deep / wide.
dig dis diip / uaid.
Excava este de hondo / ancho.
exCAva ESteh OWNdoh / AHNcho.

HANDY PHRASES   FRASES ÚTILES

Do it.
du it.
Hágalo.
AHgalo.

Don't do it.
dount du it.
No lo haga.
no lo AHga.

Do it like this.
du it laik dis.
Hágalo así.
AHgalo ahSEE.

Don't do it like that.
dount du it laik dat.
no la haga así.
no la AHga ahSEE.

Do it first / now / later.
du it furst / nau / LEIter.
Hágalo primero / ahora / más tarde.
AHgalo preMEHro / ahORa / mahs TARdeh.

Do you have enough...?
du iu jav inof...?
¿Tienes suficiente..?
¿TYEHnes soofeeceeEHNteh...?

Do you have the tools?
du iu jav de tuuls?
¿Tiene las herramientas?
¿TYEHneh lahs airaMYENtahs?

Do you know how this works?
du iu nou jau dis uerks?
¿Sabe cómo es que esto trabaja?
SAHbeh COmo ess kay EStoh traBAha?

32

Handy Phrases Frases Útiles

Do you need help?
du iu niid jelp?
¿Necesita ayuda?
neseSEEta aYOOda?

Do you understand?
du iu onderstand?
¿Entiende?
¿ehnTYEHNday?

Do you know how to do this?
du iu nou jau tu do dis?
¿Sabe cómo hacer esto?
¿SAHbeh COmo ahSAIR EStoh?

Don't waste materials.
dount ueist maTIRials.
No malgaste los materiales.
no malGAHSteh lohs matehREEAHLes.

Don't drop it.
dount drop it.
No lo deje caer.
no lo DEHheh caAIR.

Don't touch!
dount toch!
¡No toque!
¡no TOHkay!

Enough!
¡NOF!
¡Bastante!
¡baSTAHNtay!

Excuse me!
eksKIUS mi!
¡Perdón!
¡pairDOAN!

Fill / empty the bucket.
fil / EMti de BOKet.
Llena / Vacia el cubo.
YAYna / vaSEEa el COObo.

Finish the job.
FINich de chob.
Complete el trabajo.
CohmPLEHteh el traBAho.

Fix the window.
fiks de UINdou.
Arregla la ventana.
aREHgla la venTAna.

Follow the directions / signs.
FAlou de diRECchions / sains.
Siga las direcciones / señales.
SEEga lahs deerekSYOHNes / senYALes.

Frame it.
freim it.
Forma-lo.
FORma-lo.

From here to there.
from jir tu der.
de aquí a allí.
day ahKEE ah ahYEE.

HANDY PHRASES　　FRASES ÚTILES

From now on.
from nau on.
en adelante.
en ahdeLAHNtay.

Get the tools to do this.
get de tuuls tu du dis.
Trae las herramientas para hacer esto.
TRA-ay lahs airaMYENtahs PAra ahSAIR EStoh.

Get ready.
get REdi.
Prepara.
prehPAra.

Give me...
guiv mi...
Deme...
DEHmeh...

Glue the pieces.
glu de piices.
Pega los pedazos.
PEHga lohs pehDAsohs.

Go ahead / come in.
gou aHED / com in.
Adelante.
ahdeLAHNtay.

Go get the...
gou get de...
Trae el...
TRAeh el...

Go left / right / straight.
gou left / rait / streit.
Vaya a la izquierda / derecha / adelante.
VAya ah la eesKYAIRda / deREHcha / ahdeLAHNtay.

Go to the store.
gou tu de stor.
Vaya a el tienda.
VAHya ah el TYENda.

Go with him.
gou uiz jim.
Vaya con el.
VAHya cohn el.

Good job.
gud chob.
Buen trabajo.
bwain traBAho.

Grab it.
grab it.
Agárralo.
aGARralo.

Hammer it.
JAMer it.
Martillelo.
marTEEyelo.

Hang the doors.
jang de dors.
Cuélgue las puertas.
KWELLgay lahs PWAIRtas.

Handy Phrases   Frases Útiles

Have someone help you.
jav SOMuan jelp iu.
Consígue ayuda.
cohnsehGEER aYOOda.

Have you seen...?
jav iu siin...?
Has visto a...
ahss VEEstoh ah...

Help me with this.
JELP mi uiz dis.
Ayúdame con esto.
ahYOOdamay cohn ESStoh.

Here is the list.
jir is de list.
Aquí está la lista.
aKEE esTA la LEESta.

Hit it here.
jit it jiir.
Golpeélo aquí.
goalpeEHlo ahKEE.

Hold it while I cut it.
jould it uail ai cot it.
Sosténgalo mientras lo corta.
sohsTENgalo meeENtrahs lo CORta.

HANDY PHRASES   FRASES ÚTILES

How do you say...?
jau du iu sei...?
¿Cómo se dice...?
¿COmo say DEEsay...?

How does it work?
jau dos it uerk?
¿Como funciona?
¿COmo foonseeOHna?

How long will this take you?
jau long uil dis teik iu?
¿Cuánto tiempo te va tomar esto?
¿KWANtoh TYEMpo teh va tohMAR EStoh?

How much to do this?
jau moch tu du dis?
¿Cuánto para hacer esto?
¿KWANtoh PAra ahSAIR EStoh?

I am...
ai am...
Yo soy...
yo soy...

He is...
ji is...
El es...
el ess...

I can...
ai can...
Puedo...
PWEHdoh...

I can't...
ai cant...
No puedo...
no PWEHdoh...

Handy Phrases   Frases Útiles

I can do that.
ai can du dat.
Yo puedo hacer eso.
yo PWEHdoh ahSAIR ESo.

I have references / experience in...
ai jav REFerenses / eksPIRiens in...
Tengo referencias / experiencia en...
TEHNgo referenCEEahs / experienCEEa en...

I have...
ai jav...
Tengo...
TENgo...

I don't have...
ai dount jav...
No tengo...
no TENgo...

I know...
ai nou...
yo sé...
yo say...

I don't know...
ai dount nou...
No sé...
no say...

I like...
ai laik...
Me gusta...
meh GOOsta..

I don't like...
ai dount laik...
No me gusta...
no meh GOOsta...

I need...
ai niid...
Necesito...
neceSEEtoh...

I don't need...
ai dount niid...
No necesito...
no neceSEEtoh...

I need more time / money / screws.
ai niid mor taim / MOni / scruus.
Necesito mas tiempo / dinero / tornillos.
neceSEEtoh mahs TYEMpo / deeNEHro / torNEEyohs.

I understand.
ai onderSTAND.
yo comprende.
yo cohmPRENday.

I don't understand.
ai dount onderSTAND.
Yo no comprendo.
yo no comPRENdoh.

I want...
ai uant...
Yo quiero...
yo KYEERo...

I don't want...
ai dount uant...
Yo no quiero...
yo no KYEHro...

In back of...
in bak of...
Detrás de...
deTRAHS day...

In front of...
in front of...
Delante de...
deLAHNtay day...

Install the fixtures here.
instol de FIKSchurs jir.
Instala el accesorio aquí.
eenSTAla el accesoREEo ahKEE.

Insulate the walls / ceiling.
insuleit de uals / SIIlin.
Aisla las paredes / el cielo-raso.
ahEESla lahs paREHdes / el SYEHlo-RRAHso.

HANDY PHRASES

FRASES ÚTILES

It is....
it is...
Eso es...
ESo ess...

It is not...
it is not...
No es...
no ess...

It must be straight / level.
it most bi streit / LEvel.
Debe está derecho / nivelado.
DEHbeh esTAH dehREHcho / neevehLAdoh.

It's too big / too small.
its tu big / tu smol.
Es demasiado grande / pequeño.
es daymaSYAdoh GRAHNdeh / pehKAYnyo.

It works.
it uerks.
Funciona.
foonsSYOHNa.

It does not work.
it dos not uerk.
No funciona.
no foonSYOHNa.

Keep this area clean.
kiip dis EIRia cliin.
Mantenga esta área limpia.
mahnTENga ESta AHrea LEEMpya.

Knock down this wall.
nok daun dis ual.
Derribe esta pared.
dehrREEbeh esta paRED.

Handy Phrases   Frases Útiles

Lay out the frame.
lei aut de freim.
Dispona la armazón.
deesPOna la armaZONE.

Leave a message.
liiv a MESich.
Deje un mensaje.
DEHheh oon menSAheh

Let me show you how to use...
let mi chou iu jau to ius...
Permítame, a enseñarle como usar...
perMEtaymay, ah ensenYARlay ooSAR...

Lift the beam / cover.
lift de biim / COver.
Levante el viga / la tapa.
lehVAHNteh el VEEga / la TApa.

Like this.	**Not like that.**
laik dis.	not laik dat.
Así.	**Así no.**
ahSEE.	ahSEE no.
Load it.	**Unload it.**
loud it.	ONloud it.
Cárgalo.	**Descárgalo.**
CARga-lo.	DEHS-CARga-lo.

42

HANDY PHRASES   FRASES ÚTILES

Look for it.
Luk for it.
Buscalo.
BOOskalo.

Loosen / tighten the bolts.
LUsen / TAIten de bolts.
Suelte / Apriéte los pernos.
SWELLtay / ahpreeEHtay lohs PEARnohs.

Make it this size.
meik it dis sais.
Hágalo de éste tamaño.
AHgalo day ESteh taMAHNyo.

Mark a line.
mark a lain.
Marca una línea.
MARca oona LEENya.

Mix the paint / concrete.
miks de peint / CONcriit.
Mezcla la pintura / el concreto.
MESScla la peenTOOrah / el cohnCRAYtoh.

More or less.
mor or les.
Más o menos.
mahs oh MEHnohs.

Move the bricks to here.
muv de briks tu jir.
Mueve los ladrillos aquí.
MWAYveh lohs laDREEyohs ahKEE.

Nail the boards.
neil de bords.
Clava las tablas.
CLAva lahs TAblahs.

Need help?
niid jelp?
¿Necesita ayuda?
¿neceSEEta aYOOda?

Next time.
nekst taim.
la próxima vez.
la PROxima vess.

No shoes / smoking in the house.
no chuus / SMOUking in de jaus.
No se permite zapatos / fumar en la casa.
no say pairMEtay zaPAHtohs fooMAR en la CAsa.

One moment.	**On time.**
uan MOment.	on taim.
Un momento.	**A tiempo.**
oon moMENtoh.	ah TYEMpo.

Handy Phrases   Frases Útiles

Open / Close the windows.
O-pen / clous de UINdous.
Abre / Cierra las ventanas.
AHbreh / SYAIRra lahs venTAHnas.

Paint the walls.
peint de uals.
Pinta las paredes.
PEENta lahs pahREHdes.

Park here.
park jiir.
Estacione aquí.
estasyOHnay aKEE.

Patch the hole.
pach de joul.
Parcha la hoyo.
PARcha la OHjo.

Pick up the trash.
pik op de trach.
Recoja la basura.
reCOha la baSOOra.

Point to it.
point tu it.
Indícalo.
eenDEEcalo.

Handy Phrases   Frases Útiles

Push it / Pull it!
puch it / puul it!
¡Hálelo / Empujelo!
¡ahLEHlo / empooHEHlo!

Put that in the truck / trash.
put dat in de trok / trach.
Pónga eso en la troca / la basura.
POHNga ESo en la TROca / la baSOOra.

Raise / lower it a little.
reis / LOUer it a LItel.
Levántelo / Bájelo un poco.
leVAHNtelo / BAhelo oon POco.

Remove the nails / shingles.
riMUUV de neils / CHINgels.
Quita los clavos / las ripias.
KEEta lohs CLAHvohs / lahs REEpeeahs.

Repair the gate.
riPEIR de geit.
Repara el portón.
rehPAra el porTOHN.

Replace the bit.
riPLEIS de bit.
Reemplaza la broca.
reemPLAsa la BROca.

Handy Phrases　　　Frases Útiles

Return the tools.
riTURN de tuuls.
Devuélve las herramientas.
dehVWELveh lahs airaMYENtahs.

Sand this.
sand dis.
Lija esto.
LEEha EStoh.

Save the scrap.
seiv de scrap.
Salve los desperdicios.
SAHLveh lohs despehrDEEsyohs.

Scrape the wall.
screip de ual.
Raspa la pared.
RAHSpa la paRED.

Secure that.
seKIUR dat.
Asegure eso.
ahsehGOOreh ESo.

Set up the ladder / scaffold.
set op de LAder / SCAfold.
Coloca la escalera / el andamio.
coLOca la escaLEHra / el ahndaMEo.

HANDY PHRASES   FRASES ÚTILES

Shovel this into the wheelbarrow.
CHOvel dis intu de UIL-BArou
Palealo en la carretilla.
pahlehAHlo en la cahrreTEELya.

Show me.	**Show him.**
chou mi.	chou jim.
Muéstreme.	**Muéstrelo.**
MWEStraymay.	MWEStraylo.

Show me how to du this.
chou mi jau tu du dis.
Enséñeme como hacer esto.
enSEHNyeh-meh COmo AHsehr EStoh.

Spread out the plastic / gravel.
spred aut de PLAStic / GRAvel.
Esparse el plástico / la grava.
esPARseh el PLAHSteeco / la GRAva.

Stack the lumber over there.
stak de LOMber OUver der.
Apile la madera allá.
ahPEEleh la maDAYra aYA.

Stay off the grass.
stei of de gras.
No pise el césped.
no PEEsay el SESSped.

Handy Phrases   Frases Útiles

Sweep the floor.
suiip de flor.
Barra el piso.
BARra el PEEso.

Take a break / lunch
teik a breik / lonch.
Tome descanso / almuerzo.
TOHmay desCAHNso / allMWAIRso.

Take apart.   **Take down.**
teik aPART.   teik daun.
Desmonta.   **Desmantela.**
desMOANta.   desmahnTELa.

Take out the trash.
teik aut de trach.
Lleva la basura.
YEHva la baSOORa.

Take this to the trailer / dumpster.
teik dis tu de TREIler / DOMster.
Lleve esto al remolque / basurero.
YEHveh EStoh ahl reMOLLkeh / basoorAIRro.

Tell him.   **Tell me.**
tel jim.   tel mi.
Avísale.   **Avísame.**
ahVEEsalay.   ahVEEsamay.

That's enough.
dats iNOF.
Bastante.
baSTAHNtay.

There is... / There is no...
der is... / der is no...
Hay... / No hay...
I... / No I...

Tie this with cord / wire.
tai dis uiz cord / uair.
Amarre esto con cuerda / alambre.
aMARreh EStoh cohn KWAIRda / aLAHMbreh.

Tighten / loosen the fittings.
TAIten / LUsen de fitins.
Apriéte / Suelte los accesorios.
ahpreeEHtay / SWELLtay lohs ahccesoREEohs.

Turn it over / right / left.
tern it OUver / rait / left.
Voltéelo / derecha / izquierda.
volTEHelo / deREHcha / eesKYAIRda.

Turn on / off the lights.
tern on / off de laits.
Prende / apaga las luces.
PRENdeh / aPAga lahs LOOces.

Two by four (2 x 4)
tu bai for
Dos por quatro
dohs por KWAtro

Understand?
onderSTAND?
¿Entiende?
¿enTYENday?

Use this / that.
ius dis / dat.
Usa esto / eso.
OOsa EStoh / ESo.

Use this bathroom / porta - jon.
ius dis bazruum / PORta - chon.
Usar este baño / portátil.
ooSAR ESte BAHNyo / porTAteel.

Vacuum the floor.
VACjum de flor.
Aspira el piso.
ahSPEEra el PEEso.

Wash the concrete.
uach de CONcriit.
Lava el concreto.
LAva el cohnCRAYtoh.

Watch, like this.
uatch, laik dis.
Mire, asi.
MEEreh, ahSEE.

Watch your step.
uatch ior step.
Cuidado al pisar.
kweeDAdoh all peeSAR.

Wear a mask / helmet / earplugs.
uer a mask / JELmet / IIRplogs.
Usa una máscara / un casco / los tapones.
OOsa oona MAHScara / oon CAHSco /
                        lohs taPOHnes.

What does that mean?
juat dos dat miin?
¿Que quiere decir eso?.
¿kay KYAYreh deSEER ESo?

What do you want?
juat du iu uant?
¿Qué quiere?
¿kay KYEHreh?

What happened?
juat JApend?
¿Qué pasó?
¿kay paSO?

HANDY PHRASES   FRASES ÚTILES

What is that?
juat is dat?
¿Qué es eso?
¿kay ess ESSo?

What size do you need?
juat sais du iu niid?
¿Qué tamaño necesitas?
¿kay taMAHNyo neceSEEtahs?

What tools do you have?
juat tuuls du iu jav?
¿Qué herramientas tu tienes?
¿kay airaMYENtahs to TYEHnes?

What time?
juat taim?
¿Qué hora?
¿kay OHra?

What time is it?
juat taim is it?
¿Qué hora es?
¿kay OHra ess?

What's this called...?
juats dis cold...?
¿Cómo se llama esto...?
¿COmo say YAma EStoh?

When can you do it?
juen can iu du it?
¿Cuándo puede hacerlo?
¿KWANdoh PWEHdeh ahSAIRlo?

HANDY PHRASES   FRASES ÚTILES

When will you be done?
juen uil iu bi don?
¿Cuándo terminarás?
¿KWANdoh tair-meNARas?

Where is the shovel?
juer is de CHOvel?
¿Dónde está la pala?
¿DOANday esTA la PAla?

Where necessary.
juer NECEsari.
Si es necesario.
see es nesaySARyo.

Where to?
juer tu?
¿A dónde?
¿ah DOANday?

Which one?
juich uan?
¿Cuál?
¿kwall?

Why?   **Why not?**
juai?   juai not?
¿Por qué?   **¿Por qué no?**
¿por kay?   ¿por kay no?

Handy Phrases   Frases Útiles

With / Without
uiz / UIZaut
con / sin
cohn / seen

Work on this.
uerk on dis.
Trabaja en esto.
traBAha en EStoh.

You must have...
iu most jav...
Debe tener...
DEHbeh TEHnehr...

You must use / buy / finish...
iu most ius / bai / FINich...
Debe usar / comprar / acabar...
DEHbeh ooSAR / cohmPRAR / acaBAR...

You need to arrive / return / leave...
iu niid tu aRAIV / riTURN / liiv...
Necesita llegar / regresar / salir...
ncceSEEta yayGAR / regreSAR / saLEER...

You're welcome.
iour UELcom.
De nada.
deh NAda.

a	un	oon
a little	un poco	oon POco
a lot	mucho	MOOcho
a piece	un pedazo	oon peDAso
a thing	una cosa	OOna COsa
about	casi	CAsee
above	encima	enSEEma
across	a través	ah traVESS
add	suma	SOOma
addition	expansión	ekspahnseeOHN
address	dirección	deerecsyOHN
adhesive	adhesivo	ahdheSEEvo
adjust	ajustar	ahooSTAR
adjustable wrench	adjustable llave	ahdchooSTableh YAvay
after	después	desPWES
again	otra vez	OHtra vess
against	junto a	HOONtoh ah
air compressor	compressor de aire	cohmpreSOR deh I-ray
air conditioner	acondicionador de aire	ahcohn-dees-yo-naDOR de I-ray
air duct	conducto de aire	cohnDOOKtoh deh I-ray
air vent	rejilla de aire	rehHEya deh I-reh
alarm	la alarma	aLARma
all	todo	TOHdoh
alley	callejón	cayayHOAN
almost	casi	CAHsee
anchor bolt	pernos de anclaje	PAIRnohs de ahnCLAhay
and	y	ee
angle	ángulo	AHNgoolo
angle brace	cuadral	kwaDRALL
another	otro	OHtro
ants	hormigas	orMEgahs
appliance	aparato	ahpaRAtoh
application	aplicación	apleecaseeOWN

56

English	Spanish	Pronunciation
apply, to	aplicar	ahpleeCAR
appointment	cita	SEEta
appraisal	evaluación	ehvalooahSYOHN
apron	apron	ahPROAN
arches	arcos	ARcohs
architect	arquitecto	arkeeTEKtoh
Are you...?	Tiene...?	TYEHnay...?
area	área	AHreea
around	alrededor	allrehdehDOR
ask	pedir	pehDEER
asphalt	asfalto	ahsFALLtoh
assemble	juntar	hoonTAR
at	a, en	ah, en
attach, to	sujetar	sooHEHta
attic	ático	AHteeco
auger	barrena	barRAYna
awning	toldo	TOLLdoh
axe	hacha	AHcha
bad	malo	MAlo
back (move)	atrás	ahTROSS
back, backing	respaldo	resPALLdoh
bag	bolsa	BOHLsa
balcony	balcón	ballCOHN
bandage	venda	VENda
bank	banco	BAHNco
bar	la barra	BARra
bare	desnudo	dehsNOOdoh
barricade	barricada	bahreeCAda
base	base	BAsay
baseboard	zócalo	SOcalo
basement	sótano	SOtano
bathroom	baño	BAHNyo
bathtub	bañera	bahnYAIRa
batteries	las baterías	bahtairEEahs
beam	la viga	VEEga
because	porque	porKAY
bed	la cama	CAma
bedroom	recámara	rehCAmara
bees	abejas	aBAYhahs

before	antes	AHNtess
begin	empezar	empeSAR
behind	detrás de	dehTRAHS deh
below	debajo de	dehBAho deh
belt	cinturón	seentoorOHN
bench	banco	BAHNco
bend, to	doblar	dohBLAR
beside	junto a	HOONtoh ah
better, best	mejor	mehHOR
between	entre	ENtreh
bevel	cartabón	cartaBOAN
bid	oferta	ohFAIRta
big	grande	GRAHNday
bill (check)	cuenta	KWENta
bit/blade	la hoja	OH-ha
blanket	manta	MAHNta
blinds	celosías	selloSEEyahs
block	bloque	BLOkeh
blower	el soplador	soplaDOR
blueprint	anteproyecto	ahntiproYECtoh
board	la tabla	TAbla
bolt	perno	PAIRno
toggle	palanca	paLAHNca
boots	las botas	BOtahs
border	borde	BORdeh
boss	jefe	HEHfey
both	ambos	AHMbohs
bottom	fondo	FOHNdoh
box	la caja	CAha
brace	tirante	teeRAHNtay
brace, to	soportar	soporTAR
bracket	brazo	BRAHso
branch	la rama	RAma
brass	latón	laTOHN
break, (rest)	descanso	desCAHNso
break, to	romper	roamPAIR
breaker	corta-circuitos	CORta-seerKWEEtohs
brick	ladrillo	laDREEoh
bricklayer	ladrillero	ladreeYAIRoh

English	Spanish	Pronunciation
bring, to	traer	traAIR
Bring me...	Tráigame...	TRYgamay...
broken	roto	ROtoh
broom	la escoba	essCOba
brush	la brocha	BROcha
bucket	cubo	COObo
build, to	construir	cohnstrooEAR
building	edificio	edeeFEEsyo
-code	código	COdeego
-inspector	inspector	eenspecTOR
-permit	permiso	pairMEso
built-in	incorporado	eencorpoRAdoh
busy	ocupado	okooPAdoh
buy, to	comprar	cohmPRAR
C-clamp	grapa de C	GRApa deh C
cabinet	gabinete	gahbeeNEHtay
-maker	ebanista	ehbaNEEsta
cable	cable	CAbleh
call, to	llamar	yaMAR
Calm down.	Cálmase.	CALLmasay.
can	la lata	LAta
Can I...?	Puedo...?	PWEHdoh...?
Can you...?	Puede...?	PWEHdeh...?
cap	la tapa	TApa
car	carro	CArro
carbide	carburo	carBOOro
card	tarjeta	tarHEHta
cardboard	cartón	carTONE
Careful!	Cuidado!	kweeDAdoh
carpet	alfombra	allFOAMbra
carpenter	carpintero	carpeenTAIRo
carry	llevar	yayVAR
cart	carro	CArro
cash	efectivo	efecTEEvo
casing	cubierta	cooBYAIRta
caulk, to	calafatear	calafahtayAR
caulk	calafete	calaFEHteh
-gun	pistola	peeSTOla
Caution!	¡Cuidado!	kweeDAdoh!

English	Spanish	Pronunciation
ceiling	techo	TAYcho
-tile	azulejo	-ahsooLAYho
cement	cemento	sehMENtoh
center	centro	SENtro
central-heating	calefacción central	calehfaSYOHN cenTRALL
cents	centavos	cenTAvohs
ceramic tile	teja cerámica	TEHha serAHmeca
chain	cadena	caDEHna
chain saw	sierra de cadena	SYAIRra de caDEHna
chair	la silla	SEELya
chalk	tiza	TEEsa
change	cambio	CAHMbyo
change, to	cambiar	cahmBYAR
charger (batt.)	cargador	cargaDOR
cheap	barato	baRAHtoh
check (bill)	cheque	chekay
check, to	revisar	rehveeSAR
chimney	chimenea	cheemehNEHa
chisel	formón	forMOAN
chuck	mandril	mahnDREEL
circuit	circuito	seerKWEEtoh
circular saw	sierra circular	SYAIRa seercooLAR
blade	disco	DEEsco
clamp	abrazadera	ahbrasaDAIRah
clean, to	limpiar	leemPYAR
clear	claro	CLAro
clear, to	despejar	despehHAR
client	cliente	kleeINtay
climb, to	subir	sooBEER
clinic	clínica	KLEEneeka
clip	pinza	PEENsa
clippers (hedge)	las tijeras	teeHAIRahs
clogged	atorarse	ahtorARsay
close, to	cerrar	sairAR
closet	ropero	roPAIRo
cloth, a	trapo	TRApo
coat, to	cubrir	cooBREER
coffee	café	caFAY

60

English	Spanish	Pronunciation
coin	moneda	moNEHda
cold	frío	FREEyo
color	color	coLOR
column	columna	coLOOMna
come, to	ven	vehn
Come here.	Ven acá.	vehn ahCA.
complaint	lamento	laMENtoh
complete, to	completar	cohmplehTAR
component	componente	cohmpoNENtay
compound	compuesto	cohmPWEHsto
compressor	compresor	cohmpresOR
computer	computadora	cohmpootaDORa
concrete	concreto	cohnCREHtoh
-block	bloque	BLOkay
-mix	mezcla	MESScla
conduit	conducto	cohnDOOKtoh
connect, to	conectar	coneckTAR
connector	conector	coneckTOR
construction	construcción	cohnstroocSYOHN
container	recipiente	receePYENteh
continue, to	seguir	schGWEER
contract	contrato	cohnTRAtoh
contractor	contratista	cohntraTEEsta
controls	controles	cohnTROlays
copper	cobre	CObray
cord	la cuerda	CWAIRda
cordless	sin cuerda	seen CWAIRda
corner	rincón	reenCOHN
correct	correcto	corRECtoh
cost	el costo	COHsto
count, to	contar	cohnTAR
counter top	mostrador	mohstraDOR
cover	tapa	TApa
cover, to	cubrir	cooBREER
crack	la grieta	greeEHta
credit	crédito	CREHdeeto
crowbar	la barra	BARra
cup	taza	TAsa
curb	bordillo	borDEELyo
cut, to	cortar	corTAR

cutter	cortador	cortaDOR
damaged	dañado	dahnYAdoh
dangerous	peligroso	peleeGROso
dark	oscuro	ohSKOOro
date (day)	fecha	FEHcha
day	día	DEEya
day off	día libre	DEEya LEEbray
dead bolt	perno muerto	PAIRno MWAIRtoh
deck	cubierta	cooBYAIRta
decide, to	decidir	dehseeDEER
deep	hondo	OWNdoh
degree	grado	GRAdoh
delay	demora	dehMORa
den	estudio	ehstoodyo
design	diseño	deeSEHNyo
design, to	diseñar	deesehnYAR
detail	detalle	dehTAyeh
diagonal	diagonales	deeahgoNALLehs
different	diferente	deefairENtay
difficult	difícil	deeFEEseel
dig	excava	exCAva
dimmer	interruptor de amortigüar	eentair-oopTOR deh amorteeGWAR
dining room	comedor	comehDOR
dirt	la tierra	TYAIRra
dirty	sucio	SOOsyo
disconnect	desconectar	desconekTAR
dissassemble	desmontar	desmoanTAR
ditch	la zanja	SAHNha
do, to	hacer	ahSAIR
Do it.	Hágalo.	AHgahlo.
Do you have?	¿Tienes?	TYEHnehs?
Do you know?	¿Sabe?	SAbay?
Do you need?	¿Necesitas?	nehcehSEEtahs?
doctor	doctor	dohcTOR
dog	perro	PEHrro
dollar	dólares	DOHlahress
dolly	carro	CAHRro
Don't...	No...	no...

door	la puerta	PWAIRta
door bell	timbre	TEEMbray
double, to	doblar	dohBLAR
dowel	clavija	claVEEha
down	abajo	ahBAho
downspout	canelón bajo	cahneLOAN BAho
drain	desagüe	dehSAgway
drawer	gaveta	gaVEHta
drill	taladro	taLAdro
drill, to	taladrar	talaDRAR
drill bit	hoja	OHha
drink, to	tomar	tohMAR
dripping	gotear	gotehAR
drive, to	conducir	cohndoSEER
driver	chófer	CHOfehr
driveway	entrada	enTRAda
drivers license	licencia de	leecenSEEa day
	conducir	cohndooSEER
drop, to	dejar	dehHAR
drop cloth	el trapo	TRApo
dry	seco	SEHco
dry, to	secar	sehCAR
drywall	yeso	YESso
duct	conducto	cohnDOOKtoh
dump, to	tirar	teerAR
dumpster	basurero	basoorAIRo
dust	polvo	POLvo
-mask:	máscara	-MAHScara
each, every	cada	CAda
early	temprano	temPRAno
ear plugs	tapónes de oído	taPOnes de oEdoh
earth	tierra	TYAIRa
easy	fácil	FAseel
eat, to	comer	coMEHR
eaves	aleros	aLAIRohs
edge	borde	BORday
edger	caladora	calaDORa
electric	eléctrico	ehLECtreeco
-cord	extensión	extenseeOWN

English	Spanish	Pronunciation
electrician	electricista	electreeSEEsta
Email	Dirección electrónica	DeerekSYOHN ehlekTROneeka
emergency	emergencia	ehmairHENsya
employ, to	emplear	emplayAR
empty	vacío	vaSYO
empty, to	vaciar	vaSYAR
end, tip	fin	feen
engineer	ingeniero	eenhenYAYro
Enough.	Bastante.	bahsTAHNtay
Enough?	¿Suficiente?	soofeeceeENtay?
enter, to	entrar	enTRAR
entrance	entrada	enTRAda
equipment	equipo	ehKWEEpo
estimate	estimado	ehsteeMAdoh
even	plano	PLAno
everybody	todo el mundo	TOHdoh el MOONdoh
everyday	diario	DYARyo
everything	todo	TOHdoh
excuse me	perdón	pairDOAN
exit	salida	saLEEda
expensive	caro	CAro
explain, to	explicar	expleeCAR
exterior	exterior	extaireeOR
eyes	ojos	OHhohs
-protection	protección	protecSYOHN
facade	fachada	faCHAda
face shield	escudo (cara)	esCOOdoh (CAra)
fall, to	caer	caEHR
fan	ventilador	venteelaDOR
fascia	faja	FAha
fast	rápido	RApeedoh
fastener	asegura	ahsehGOOra
faucet	la llave	YAveh
felt (roof)	asfálta	ahsFALta
fence	la cerca	SAIRka
fertilize	abonar	ahboNAR
few	poco	POco

file	lima	LEEma
file, to	limar	leeMAR
fill, to	llenar	yehNAR
fill out (form)	completar	cohmplehTAR
final	final	feeNAL
find, to	buscar	booSCAR
fine (grain)	fino	FEEno
finger	dedo	DEEdoh
finish (surface)	acabado	acaBAdoh
finish, to	completar	cohmplehTAR
fire	fuego	FWEH go
fire, to	terminar	tehrmeNAR
fire extinguisher	extintor de fuego	exTEENtor de FWEHgo
fireplace	chimenea	cheemehNAYa
first aid	primeros auxilios	preeMAIRohs aukSEALyohs
first floor	primer piso	PREEmehr PEEso
fit, to	ajustar	ahhooSTAR
fitting	accesorio	ahccessORyo
fix, to	arreglar	arrehGLAR
fixture	artículo	arTEEcoolo
flashing	tapajuntas	tapaHOONtahs
flashlight	linterna	leenTAIRna
flat	plano	PLAno
float, to	flotar	floTAR
floor	piso	PEEso
floor plan	plano de suelo	plahno deh swehlo
flooring	entablado	entaBLAdoh
flowers	flores	FLOREs
foam	espuma	esPOOma
follow, to	seguir	sehGWEER
Follow me.	Sígame.	SEEgameh.
foot	pie	pyeh
for	para, por	PAra, por
foreman	el capataz	cahpaTAHS
form (mold)	molde	MOHLdeh
form (paper)	formulario	formooLARyo
forward	adelante	ahdehLAHNtay
foundation	fundación	foondaSYOHN
fountain	la fuente	FWENtay

fragil	**frágil**	FRAheel
frame	**armazón**	armaZONE
frame, to	**enmarcar**	ehnmarCAR
freezing	**congelando**	cohngeLAHNdoh
friend	**amigo**	aMEgo
from	**de**	deh
front	**frente**	FRENteh
fruit	**la fruta**	FROOta
fuel	**combustible**	cohmbooSTEEblay
full	**lleno**	YAYno
funnel	**embudo**	emBOOdoh
furniture	**los muebles**	MWEHbless
fuse	**fusible**	fooSEEblay
gable	**aguilón**	ahgweeLOAN
gallon(s)	**galón(es)**	gaLOn(es)
garage	**garaje**	gaRAhay
garbage	**la basura**	baSOOra
garden	**el jardín**	harDEEN
gardener	**jardinero**	hardeeNAYro
gas (natural)	**gas**	gahs
gasoline	**la gasolina**	gahsoLEEna
gate	**portón**	porTONE
gauge (width)	**calibre**	caLEEbray
gauge (dial)	**indicador**	eendeeCAdor
generator	**generador**	hehnehRAdor
get, to	**conseguir**	cohnsehGWEER
Get the...	**Consiga...**	cohnSEEga...
Get ready.	**Prepara.**	prehPARa
girder	**viga**	VEEga
Give me it.	**Démelo.**	DAYmehlo.
glass	**vidrio**	VEEdreeo
gloves	**los guantes**	GWANtes
glue	**la goma**	GOma
glue, to	**pegar**	pehGAR
glue gun	**arma de goma**	ARma deh GOma
Go.	**VAya.**	VAya.
Go get...	**Traer...**	traEHR
Go back.	**Regresar.**	rehgressAR
goggles	**anteojos**	ahnteeOHhohs

goma	rubber	RAber
good	bueno	BWAYno
goodbye	adiós	ahdeeOHS
gouges	formones	forMOANess
grab, to	agarrar	ahgarRAR
Grab it.	Agárralo..	ahGARralo.
grade	grado	GRAdoh
grain (wood)	veta	VEHta
granite	granito	graNEEtoh
gravel	la grava	GRAva
grease	la grasa	GRAsa
green card	tarjeta verde	tarhehta VAIRday
grinder	amolador	ahmolaDOR
grind, to	amolar	ahmolAR
groove	ramura	raMOOra
ground	suelo	SWAYlo
grout	lechada	lehCHAda
guarantee	garantía	garanTEEa
guardrail	la baranda	baRAHNda
gutter	canelón	cahneLOAN
hack saw	sierra metales	SYAIRa mcTALes
half	medio	MAIDyo
hall	pasillo	paSEEyo
hammer	el martillo	marTEEyo
hand	la mano	MAHno
handsaw	cerrucho	sairROOcho
handle	mango	MAHNgo
hand truck	carro de mano	CARro de MAno
hang, to	colgar	coalGAR
hanger	colgante	coalGAHNtay
hard	duro	DOOro
hard hat	casco	CAHSco
hardware	ferreteria	fairetairEEa
hardware store	la ferretería	fairetairEEa
hardwood	madera	maDAIRa
	o dura	o DOra
harness	arneses	arNESes
hatchet	hacha	AHcha
haul, to	jala	HAla

English	Spanish	Pronunciation
hazardous	peligroso	peleeGROso
he	el	el
head	cabeza	caBAYsa
header	cabezal	cahbehSAL
heat	calor	caLOR
heater	calentador	calentaDOR
heating	calefacción	calefaSYOHN
heavy	pesado	pehSAdoh
helmet	casco	CAHSco
Help!	¡Soccoro!	¡soCORro!
help, to	ayudar	ayooDAR
Help me.	Ayúdame.	aYOOdamay.
her	ella	ELla
here	aquí	ahKEE
high	alto	ALLtoh
high voltage	alto voltaje	ALLtoh volTAhay
him	le, lo	leh, lo
hinge	la bisagra	beeSAgra
hire, to	emplear	emplehAR
his	su	soo
hit, to	golpear	golpehAR
hoe	azadón	ahsaDOHN
hoe, to	azadonar	ahsadohNAR
hoist	alzamiento	alsaMYENtoh
hold, to	sostener	sohstenEHR
hole	hoyo	OHho
hook	gancho	GAHNcho
horizontal	horizontal	oreeSOHNtahl
hose	la manguera	mahnGWAIRa
hospital	hospital	ohspeeTAL
hot	caliente	calYENtay
hour	hora	OHra
house	la casa	CAsa
How?	¿Como?	COmo?
How many?	¿Cuántos?	KWANtohs?
How much?	¿Cuánto?	KWANtoh?
hungry	hambre	AHMbray
Hurry up!	¡Dese prisa!	DEHseh PREEsa!
Hurt?	¿Herido?	ehREEdoh?

English	Spanish	Pronunciation
I	Yo	yo
I am...	Yo soy...	yo soy...
I can...	Puedo...	PWEHdo...
I can't...	No puedo...	no PWEHdo..
I charge...	Yo cobro...	yo CObro...
I have...	Tengo...	TENgo...
I know...	Yo sé...	yo say...
I like...	Me gusta...	meh GOOsta...
I need...	Necesito...	nehsehSEEtoh...
I want...	Yo quiero...	yo KYEERo...
I'm	Soy	soy
I'm busy.	Estoy ocupado.	esTOY okooPAdoh.
I'm going.	Yo voy.	yo voy.
I'm sorry.	Lo siento.	lo SYENtoh
identification	identificación	eeden-teefee-caSYOHN
important	importante	eemporTAHNtay
in	en	en
in back of	detrás de	dehTRAHS day
in front of	en frente de	en FREHNtay day
inches	pulgadas	poolGAdas
incorrect	incorrecto	eencorRECtoh
injury	lesión	lehseeOHN
insect	insecto	eenSECtoh
insecticide	insecticida	eensecteeSEEda
inside	adentro	aDENtro
inside of	dentro de	DEHNtro day
inspector	inspector	eenspecTOR
install, to	instalar	eenstaLAR
instantly	al punto	ahl poontoh
instructions	instrucciones	een-strook-seeOWNes
insulate, to	aislar	ice-LAR
insulation	aislamiento	ice-laMYENtoh
insurance	seguros	seGOORohs
-liability	-responsabilidad	responsabiliDAHD
interior	interior	eentaireeOR
interpret, to	interpretar	eentairprcTAR
interpreter	traductor	tradookTOR
into	dentro	DENtro

English	Spanish	Pronunciation
into the	adentro de	aDENtro day
invoice	factura	fahcTOOra
is	es	ess
it	lo	lo
It costs...	Cuesta...	KWESta...
It works.	Funciona.	foonseeOWNa
jack	gato	GAtoh
jack hammer	perfordora	perforDORa
jack stands	base para el gato	BAsay PAra el GAtoh
jamb	jamba	HAHMba
jig	plantilla	plahnTEEya
job	trabajo	traBAho
job site	sitio de trabajo	SEEteeo de traBAho
joint	unión	ooneeOWN
-compound	la macia	maSEEya
joist	vigueta	veGEHta
keep, to	guardar	gwarDAR
Keep it.	Guárdelo.	GWARdelo.
Keep out.	No entre.	no EHNtray.
kerosene	querosén	cairoSEHN
key	la llave	YAvay
kitchen	la cocina	coSEEna
knife	cuchillo	coCHEEo
-utility knife	utilitario	ooteeleeTARyo
Knock down.	Derribar.	dairyBAR
knob	pomo	POmo
lacquer	laca	LAca
ladder	la escalera	eskaLAIRa
lamp	la lámpara	LAHMpara
land	tierra	TYAIRa
landscape	paisaje	pieSAhay
landscaper	paisajero	pie-saHAIRo
large	grande	GRAHNday
last	último	OOLteemo
latch	cierre	SYAIReh
late	tardío	tarDEEo

later	más tarde	mahs TARday
lawn	el césped	SESped
lawnmower	cortacésped	cortaCESSped
lay, to	poner	poNEHR
lay out	acostar	ahcoSTAR
leak	gotera	goTEHRa
learn, to	aprender	ahprenDEHR
leave, to (drop)	dejar	dehHAR
leave, to (exit)	salir	saLEER
leaves	hojas	OHhahs
left	izquierda	eesKWAIRda
less	menos	MEHnohs
Let's go.	Vámonos.	VAmanohs
level, to	nivelar	neevelAR
Level it.	Nivelo.	Neeveloh
level (tool)	nivel	NEEvel
lever	la palanca	paLANca
license	licencia	leecenSEEa
lid	la tapa	TApa
lift, to	levantar	lchvahnTAR
lightbulb	la bombilla	bohmBEEya
light (color)	claro	CLAro
light (weight)	ligero	leeGEHRo
lights	las luces	lahs LOOSEs
Like this.	Así.	ahSEE
lime	cal	cahl
line	la línea	LEEnaya
linoleum	linóleo	leeNOleho
list	lista	LEESta
Listen!	¡Escuche!	esKOOchay!
little	poco	POco
livingroom	la sala	SAla
load, to	cargar	carGAR
lock	la cerradura	sayraDOOra
lock, to	cerrar	sairAR
long	largo	LARgo
look, to	buscar	booSCAR
Look for...	Busca...	BOOsca...
loose	suelto	SWELtoh
loosen, to	soltar	soulTAR

English	Spanish	Pronunciation
lost	perdido	pairDEEdoh
lot	parcela	parSELa
low	bajo	BAho
lower	más bajo	mahs BAho
lumber	la madera	maDAYra
lunch	almuerzo	allMWAIRso
machine	la máquina	MAkeena
magnet	imán	eeMAHN
mahogany	caoba	caOba
mailbox	buzón	booZONE
main	principal	preenseePALL
maintain, to	mantener	mahntehNEHR
make, to	hacer	ahSEHR
mallet	mazo	MAso
man	hombre	OHMbray
many	muchos	MOOchohs
map	mapa	MApa
marble	mármol	MARmole
mark, to	marcar	marCAR
market	mercado	mairCAdoh
mask	máscara	MAHScahra
masking tape	cinta enmascar	seenta enMAHScar
mason	albañil	allbahnYEEL
masonite	masonita	mahsoNEEta
mastic	mástique	MAHSteekay
match, to	emparejar	emparehHAR
matches	los fósforos	lohs FOsforohs
material	material	matehrYAL
maybe	quizás	keeSAHS
May I...?	Puedo...?	PWEHdoh...?
me	yo	jo
measure, to	medir	mehDEER
Measure it.	Mídelo.	MEEdelo.
measuring tape	cinta de medir	ceenta de meDEER
mechanic	mecánico	mehCAneeco
meet, to	encontrar	enconTRAR
medicine	medicina	medeeCEEna
message	mensaje	menSAheh
metal	metal	mehTAL
-sheet:	hoja	OHha

English	Spanish	Pronunciation
meter (dial)	medidor	mehdeeDOR
middle	medio	MAIDyo
mile	milla	MEELya
minute	minuto	meNOOtoh
mine	mio	MEEoh
mirror	espejo	esPEHho
miter box	caja de ingletes	CAha deh eenGLEHtehs
mix	mezcla	MESScla
mixer	mezcladora	mesclaDOHra
mold (fungus)	moho	MOho
molding	moldura	mohlDOOra
money	dinero	deeNAYro
money order	giro postal	geero postall
month	mes	mess
mop	trapeador	trahpayaDOR
more	más	mahs
morning	mañana	mahnYAna
mortar	mortero	morTAIRo
move, to	mover	mohVAIR
mow, to	cortar	corTAR
Mrs./ma'am	señora	senYORa
much	mucho	MOOcho
mud	lodo	LOdoh
mulch	cubrir con paja	cooBREER cohn PAha
my	mi	me
nail, to	clavar	claVAR
nail gun	clavadora	clavaDORa
nail puller	sacaclavos	sacaCLAvohs
nails	clavos	CLAvohs
narrow	agosto	ahGOStoh
name	nombre	NOHMbreh
near	cerca de	SAIRca deh
need, to	necesitar	neceseeTAR
needle	aguja	ahGOOha
never	nunca	NOONca
new	nuevo	NWEHvo
next	próximo	PROHXeemo
next to	al lado de	all LAdoh deh

73

night	noche	NOchay
no	no	no
no smoking	no fumar	no fooMAR
nobody	nadie	NAHDyeh
none	ninguno	neenGOOno
noon	mediodía	mehdyoDEEa
not	no	no
Not bad	no está mal	no esTA mall
Not now	ahora no	ahORa no
Not yet	todavía no	tohdaVEEa no
nothing	nada	NAda
notch	muesca	MWESSca
now	ahora	ahORa
nozzle	la boquilla	la boKEEa
number	número	NOOmayro
nut	la tuerca	la TWAIRca
oak	roble	RObleh
of	de	deh
off	apagado	ahpaGAdoh
office	la oficina	ofeeSEEna
oil	el aceite	el ahSYEHtay
old	viejo	VYAYho
on	en	en
on time	a tiempo	ah TYEMpo
on top of	sobre	SObreh
one by four	uno por cuatro	OOno por KWAtro
one moment	un momento	oon moMENtoh
once	una vez	OOna vess
once more	otra vez	O-tra vess
only	solamente	solaMENtay
open	abierto	ahBYAIRtoh
open, to	abrir	ahBREER
operate, to	operar	ohpairAR
opposite	opuesto	ohPWEStoh
or	o	o
order, to	ordenar	ordehNAR
other, the	otro, el	O-tro
other side	otro lado	O-tro LAdoh
out	fuera	FWAIRa

out of order	no sirve	no SEERvay
outlets	enchufes	enCHOOfess
outside	afuera	ahFWAIRa
over	encima	enSEEma
over there	allá	allYA
overflow	derramarse	derraMARsay
overhang	la proyección	proyecSYOHN
overlap	traslapo	trahsLApo
owner	dueño	DWAYno
paint	la pintura	la peenTOOra
paint, to	pintar	peenTAR
paint thinner	aguarrás	ahgwarAHS
pallet	la paleta	paLAYta
pan	la cacerola	caseh ROla
pane	cristal	creeSTALL
panel	el panel	el paNEL
paneling	empanelado	empahneLAdoh
paper	papel	paPEL
parapet	parapeto	pahraPETo
park, to	estacionar	estahsyoNAR
part	la parte	PARteh
particle board	tabla de partícula	TAbla deh parTEEcoola
partition	separación	separahSYOHN
patch	el parche	el PARchay
patch, to	emparchar	emparCHAR
patio	el patio	PAtyo
pavement	pavimento	paveeMENtoh
pay	paga	PAga
pay, to	pagar	paGAR
pay day	diá de pago	DEEya de PAgo
paycheck	el cheque	CHEkay
pen	pluma	PLOOma
pencil	la lápiz	LApees
phillips head	punta de cruz	POONta de croos
phone	teléfono	teLEHfono
pick (tool)	pico	PEEko
pick up, to	recoger	rehco HER
piece	pedazo	pehDAso

English	Spanish	Pronunciation
pile	pila	PEEla
pile, to	apilar	ahpeeLAR
pin	alfiler	allFEEler
pint	pinta	PEENta
pipe	tubo	TOObo
piping	tubería	toobehrEEa
pipe wrench	llave de tubo	YAYveh de TOObo
plane (tool)	cepillo	sehPEEyo
plans	planos	PLAnohs
plant(s)	las plantas	PLAHNtas
plant, to	sembrar	semBRAR
planter	maceta	maSAYtahs
plaster	yeso	YEHso
plastic	plástico	PLAHSteeco
plate	plato	PLAtoh
please	por favor	por faVOR
pliers	alicates	aleeCAtehs
-channel lock	de extensión	day extenSYOHN
plug	enchufe	enCHOOfeh
plumb	plomada	ploMAda
plumb (vertical)	a plomo	ah PLOmo
plumb bob	el plomo	PLOmo
plumber	plomero	ploMAIRo
plumbing	plomería	plomairEEo
plunger	sopapa	soPApa
plywood	madera laminada	maDAIRa lameeNAda
pocket	bolsillo	bolSEEyo
Point to...	Indicar...	eendeeCAR...
poison	veneno	vehNAYno
polish, to	pulir	pooLEER
pool	la piscina	peeSEENa
porch	el porche	PORchay
portable	portátil	porTAteel
porta-jon	portátil	porTAteel
post	poste	POHSteh
pound(s)	libra (s)	LEEbra (s)
powder	el polvo	POLvo
power tool	herramienta electrica	airraMYENta ehlecTREEca

English	Spanish	Pronunciation
pressure	presión	prehSYOHN
-wash	lavar	laVAR
price	precio	preSEEo
primer	pintura de base	peenTOra deh BAsay
Private.	Privado.	preeVAdoh
problem	problema	proBLEHma
project	proyecto	proYECtoh
pronounce, to	pronunciar	pronoonSYAR
property	propiedad	propyaDAHD
protection	protección	protecSYOHN
prune, to	podar	poDAR
pry-bar	la barra	BARra
pull, to	Halar	ahLAR
pump	la bomba	BOHMba
punch	punzones	poonSOness
purchase order	orden de	orDEHN deh
	compra	COHMpra
push, to	empujar	empooHAR
put, to	poner	poNEHR
Put it...	Póngalo...	POHNgalo...
Put away...	Guarda...	GWARda...
putty	masilla	maSEEya
-knife	-espátula	-esPAtoola
quarter 1/4	cuarto	KWARtoh
question, to	preguntar	pregoonTAR
quickly	pronto	PROHNtoh
radial saw	sierra fija	SYAIRa FEEha
radio	radio	RAdyo
rafter	cabrio	CAbreeo
rag	trapo	TRAHpo
railing	la baranda	baRAHNda
rain	lluvia	YOOvya
raise, to	levantar	levahnTAR
rake	rastrillo	raSTREEyo
rake, to	rastrillar	rastreeAR
ramp	la rampa	RAHMpa
ratchet	trinquete	treenKEHteh
read, to	leer	lehAIR

Read this.	**Lea esto.**	LEHa EStoh.
ready	listo	LEEsto
rebajador	router	RAUTer
re-bar	varilla	vaREEyah
receipt	recibo	rehSEEbo
recently	recientemente	rehsyenteMENteh
reciprocating saw (sawsall)	reciprocar sierra	reseeproCAR SYAIRa
redondo	round	raund
referral	referencia	rehferehnSEEah
refrigerator	refrigerador	rehfreeheraDOR
reinforced	refuerzo	rehFWEHRso
remove, to	quitar	keeTAR
repair, to	reparar	rehpaRAR
repairman	reparador	rehparaDOR
Repeat!	**¡Repita!**	rayPEEta!
replace, to	reemplazar	rehemplaSAR
respirator	respirador	respeeraDOR
rest, to	descansar	descahnSAR
return, to	devolver	devolVEHR
return (come back)	regresar	raygraySAR
reverse	reverso	rehVEHRso
ridge	cresta	CRESSta
right	derecha	dehREHcha
right angle	angulo recto	angoolo recto
Right now	**ahora mismo**	ahORa MEESmo
road	camino	caMEno
rocks	las rocas	ROkahs
rod	la vara	VARa
roll up, to	enrollar	enroYAR
roller	el rodillo	roDEEyo
roof	el techo	TEHcho
roof felt	la felpa	la FELLpa
roofer	techero	tehCHAIRo
room	el cuarto	KWARtoh
root	raíz	raEESS
rope	la soga	SOga
rough	áspera	AHSpaira
rough ins	mano gruesa	MAno GROOaysa
round	redondo	rehDOHNdoh

English	Spanish	Pronunciation
router	rebajador	rehbahaDOR
rubber	goma	GOma
rugs	tapetes	taPEHtehs
saddle	montura	moanTOOra
safety	seguridad	sehgooreeDAHD
-glass	vidrio	VEEdreeo
-glasses	gafas	GAfass
-harness	arneses	arNESSes
-line	la linea	la LEEneha
-rails	pasamanos	pasaMAHNohs
same	mismo	MEESmo
sand	la arena	ahREEna
sand, to	lijar	leeHAR
sander	lijadora	leehaDORa
sand paper	papel de lija	paPEL deh LEEha
sanding disc	disco de arena	DEEsco de aREna
save, to	ahorrar	ahorRAR
saw	sierra	SYAIRra
-blade	la hoja	la OHha
saw horse	burro, carp	BOORro, carp
say, to	decir	dehSEER
scaffold	andamio	ahnDAmyo
schedule	horario	ohRAreeo
scissors	tijeras	teeHAIRahs
screen	biombo	beeOHMbo
scrap	desperdicios	dehspairDEEsyohs
scrape, to	raspar	rahsPAR
scraper	rascador	rascaDOR
screw	tornillo	torNEEyo
-gun	pistola	peesTOHla
-jacks	nivela	neeVELa
screw, to	atornillar	atorneeYAR
screw driver	destornillador	destor-neeyaDOR
-flat head	plano	PLAno
-phillips	cruz	crooss
seal	la unión	la ooneeOWN
seal, to	sellar	sehYAR
sealant	sellante	sehYAHNtay
seat	el asiento	ahSYENtoh

second	segundo	sehGOONdoh
section	sección	secSYOHN
secure, to	asegurar	ahsehgooRAR
see	ver	vehr
seed, to	semillero	semeeYAIRo
send, to	mandar	mahnDAR
separate, to	separar	sehpaRAR
septic tank	pozo séptico	POtho SEPteeco
service panel	panel de servicio	pahNEL de serVEEsyo
set up, to	alzar	allZAR
sewer	alcantarilla	alcantaREEya
she	ella	ELla
shears	tijeras grande	teeHAIRahs grande
shed	cobertizo	coberTEEso
sheet	la hoja	OHha
sheet rock	tabla roca	TAbla ROca
shelf	ripisa	rehPEEsa
shim	calce	CALsay
shingles	las ripias	reePEEahs
short	corto	CORtoh
shovel	la pala	PAla
shovel, to	palear	palehAR
shovelful	palada	paLAda
show, to	mostrar	moSTRAR
Show me.	Muéstreme.	MWEStraymay.
shower	la ducha	DOcha
shut, to	cerrar	sehrAR
shutters	contraventanas	cohntra-venTAnahs
sick	enfermo	enFAIRmo
side	lado	LAdoh
sidewalk	acera	aSEHra
siding	apartadero	apartaDEHRo
signs, signals	las señales	senYALess
sign, to	firmar	fearMAR
Sign here.	Firme aqui.	FEARmay ahKEE.
sill	antepecho	ahntePEHcho
similar	similar	seemeeLAR
sink	lavadero	lavaDEHro
sir	señor	senYOR
Sit down.	Siéntate.	SYENtatay.

site	sitio	SEEtyo
size	tamaño	taMAHNyo
skylight	tragaluz	tragaLOOS
slab	la losa	LOsa
sledgehammer	acotillo	ahcoTEEyo
sleeve	manga	MAHNga
slide, to	deslizar	desleeSAR
-bolt	perno	PEHRno
-door	puerta	PWAIRta
slope	cuesta	KWESta
Slow down.	Más despacio.	mahs deSPAsyo.
slowly	despacio	desPAsyo
small	pequeño	pehKENyo
smaller	mas pequeño	mahs pehKENyo
smoke detector	sensor de humo	senSOR de OOmo
smoking	fumar	fooMAR
soap	jabón	haBONE
social security	seguro social	seGOOro soSYAL
-card	tarjeta	tarHEHta
socket	hueco	ooEHco
socket wrench	llave hueco	YAYvay ooEHco
soffit	sofito	soFEEtoh
soft	blando	BLAHNdoh
soil	la tierra	la TYAIRra
solder	soldadura	souldaDOOra
solderer	soldador	souldaDOR
solid	sólido	SOleedoh
some	algo	ALLgo
something	alguna cosa	allGOOna COsa
sometimes	alguna veces	allgoona VEHsehs
soon	pronto	PROHNtoh
sorry	lo siento	lo SYENtoh
spackle	yeso	YEHso
speak, to	hablar	ahBLAR
spell, to	deletrear	dehlehtrayAR
sponge	la esponja	essPOHNha
spray, to	rociar	roseeAR
-gun	pistola	peeSTOla
sprayer	rociadora	roseeaDORa
spread, to	esparcir	esparSEER

sprinkler	rociador	roceeahDOR
square	cuadrado	kwaDRAdoh
square (tool)	escuadra	esKWAdra
square foot	pie cuadrado	pyeh kwadradoh
square yard	yarda " "	IARda " "
stack, to	apilar	ahpeeLAR
stake	estaca	esTAca
stain (wood)	tintura	teenTOOra
stain (mess)	mancha	MAHNcha
stairs	escaleras	eskaLEHra
standard	estándar	essTAHNdar
stapler	engrapadora	engrapaDORa
staple	la grapa	GRAHpa
-gun	pistola	peeSTOla
start, to	empezar	empyehSAR
Start at...	Empieza a las	emPYEHsa a lahs...
stay, to	quedar	kayDAR
steel	acero	ahSEHro
steps	escalones	escaLOnehs
stick	palo	PAlo
stone	piedra	PYEHdra
Stop!	Pare!	PAreh!
Stop at...	Para en la...	PAra en la...
storage	depósito	dehPOseetoh
store	tienda	TYENda
story (floor)	piso	PEEso
straight	derecho	deREHcho
straightedge	la regla	REHgla
strap	la banda	BAHNda
street	la calle	CAyay
string	cuerda	KWAIRda
strong	fuerte	FWAIRteh
stucco	estuco	ehSTOOko
stud	montante	mohnTAHNtay
stud finder	buscador	booscaDOR
stump	el tocón	el tohCOHN
subcontractor	subcontratista	soobcohntraTEEsta
sun	sol	soul
support	soporta	soPORta
support, to	soportar	soporTAR

English	Spanish	Pronunciation
surface	superficie	sooperFEEsyee
sweep, to	barrer	baRAIR
swimming pool	la piscina	la peeSEEna
switch	interruptor	eentair-oopTOR
T-square	regla T	REHgla Tee
table	la mesa	MEHsa
table saw	sierra de mesa	SYAIRa de MEHsa
tack	tachuela	tachooELa
take	tomar	tohMAR
take apart, to	desmontar	desmoanTAR
take away, to	sacar	saCAR
tall	alto	ALLtoh
tank	tanque	TAHNkay
tape	cinta	SEENta
tape, to	encintar	ehnseenTAR
tape measure	cinta metro	SEENta MEHtro
tapetcs	rugs	rags
tar	la brea	la BRAYa
tar paper	papel de brea	paPEL deh BRAYa
tarp	la lona	LOna
tax	impuesto	eemPWEStoh
-form	formulario	formooLARyo
-federal	federales	fedeRAles
-state	estatales	estaTAHles
telephone	telélfono	tehLEHfono
tell, to	decir	dehSEER
Tell me.	Dígame.	DEEgamay.
temperature	temperatura	temperaTOOra
tempered glass	vidrio templado	veedreeo templado
terminate, to	terminar	tairmeeNAR
termites	termitas	tairMEtahs
test, to	probar	proBAR
thanks	gracias	GRAsyus
that	eso	ESso
that's all	eso es todo	ESoh ess TOHdoh
the	el, la	el, la
(plural):	los, las	lohs, lahs
then	entonces	enTOHNsess
them	los	lohs

there	allí	allYEE
There is...	Hay...	I...
these	estos	ESStohs
they	ellos	ELyohs
thin	delgado	delGAdoh
thing	cosa	COsa
think, to	pensar	pehnSAR
thirsty	sed	sed
this	este	ESSteh
those	esos	ESSohs
thousand	mil	meel
through	a través de	ah traVES deh
throw, to	tirar	teeRAR
tie, a	lazo	LAso
tie, to	atar	ahTAR
tie downs	lazo abajo	LAso aBAho
tight	apretado	ahprehTAdoh
tighten, to	apretar	ahprehTAR
tile (roof)	la teja	TAYha
tile (floor)	baldosa	ballDOHsa
tile (ceramic)	azulejo	asooLAYho
-cutter	cortador	cortaDOR
-pliers	alicates	ahleeCAtess
time	tiempo	TYEMpo
Time?	¿Qué hora?	kay OHra?
time sheet	hoja de tiempo	OHa deh TYEMpo
tin	la lata	LAta
tin snips	tijeras de lata	teeHAIRahs deh LAta
tip	la punta	POONta
tired	cansado	cahnSAdoh
to	a	ah
today	hoy	oy
together	juntos	HOONtohs
toggle bolt	palanca perno	paLANca PAIRno
toilet	excusado	excooSAdoh
tomorrow	mañana	mahnYAna
ton	tonelada	tohnehLAda
Too much!	¡Demasiado!	dehmaseeAHdoh

English	Spanish	Pronunciation
tool	herramienta	airaMYENta
-belt	cinturón	seentooROAN
-box	caja	CAha
top	tope	TOHpay
top (lid)	tapa	TApa
touch, to	tocar	tohCAR
trailer	el remolque	rehMOHLkay
Translate.	Traduce.	traDOOsay.
translator	traductor	tradookTOR
transportation	transportación	transportahSYOHN
trap	sifón	seeFOHN
trash	basura	baSOOra
-bag	bolsa	BOLsa
-can	cubo	COObo
tree	árbol	ARbowl
trellis	enrejado	enrehHAdoh
trench	la zanja	SANha
trim	moldura	moleDOOra
trim, to	recortar	recorTAR
trowel	la paleta	paLEHta
truck	el camión	caMYOHN
truckdriver	camionero	camyoNAIRo
truss	armadura	armaDOOra
try, to	tratar	traTAR
tub	la bañera	bahnYAIRa
tube	el tubo	TOObo
turn, to	voltear	vohltehAR
turn off	apagar	ahpaGAR
turn on	encender	ensanDAIR
twice	dos veces	VEHsehs
twist, to	torcer	torSAIR
two by four	dos por cuatro	dohs por KWAtro
two by six	dos por seis	dohs por sayss
uncover, to	descubrir	dehscooBREER
under	debajo de	dehBAho deh
-ground	subterráneo	soobteRAHneo
understand, to	entender	entenDAIR
undo	deshacer	des-haSAIR
uneven	desigual	dehSEEgwal

English	Spanish	Pronunciation
uniform	el uniforme	ooneeFORmay
union (group)	sindicato	seendeeCAHtoh
unit	unidad	ooneeDAHD
United States	Estados Unidos	esTAdohs ooNEEdohs
unload, to	descargar	descarGAR
unroll, to	desenrollar	desenroYAR
untie, to	desatar	desahTAR
up	arriba	aREEba
upstairs	arriba	aREEba
us	nosotros	noSOtrohs
use, to	usar	ooSAR
utilities	utilidades	ooteeleeDAdahs
vacuum, to	aspirar	ahspeerAR
-cleaner	aspiradora	ahspeeraDORa
valley	valle	VAyay
valve	la válvula	VALLvoola
vegetable	vegetal	vehehTAL
vehicle	el vehículo	vehHEcoolo
veneer	chapa	CHApa
vent	respiradero	rehspee-raDAIRo
ventilate, to	ventilar	venteeLAR
vertical	vertical	vehrteeCALL
very	muy	MOOee
vine	la vid	veed
violet	violete	veeohLEHta
vise	torno	TORno
vise grips	llaves tornos	YAYvess TORnohs
volt	voltio	vohlTEEo
-110	ciento diez	SYENtoh DEEess
-220	doscientos-veinte	dohSYENtohs-VAINtay
Wait!	¡Espere!	essPEHreh!
walk, to	andar	ahnDAR
walkway	la acera	la aSAYra
wall	la pared	paRED
wallpaper	empapelado	empapeLAdoh
want, to	querer	kayRAIR

warehouse	el almacén	allmaSEHN
wash, to	lavar	laVAR
washer	la arandela	ahrahnDELLa
waste, to	malgastar	mallgahsTAR
watch, to	mirar	meeRAR
water	agua	AHgwa
-drinking	potable	poTAblay
-filter	filtro	FEELtro
-meter	medidor	mehdeeDOR
water, to	regar	rehGAR
water heater	calentador de agua	calentaDOR de AHgwa
wax	la cera	SAIRa
we	nosotros	noSOtrohs
wear, to	llevar	yehVAR
weather	tiempo	TYEMpo
-stripping	burletes	boorLETess
wedge	la cuña	COONya
weeds	yerbajos	jairBAhohs
week	semana	sehMAna
weight	peso	PEHso
welcome	bienvenidos	byenvehNEEdohs
weld, to	soldar	soulDAR
wet	mojado	moHAdoh
What?	¿Qué?	kay?
What's this?	¿Qué es esto?	kay ess ESStoh?
What time?	¿Qué hora?	kay OHra?
wheel barrow	la carretilla	cahrrehTEEya
When?	¿Cuándo?	KWANdoh?
Where?	¿Dónde?	DOANday?
Where is?	¿Donde está?	DOANday esTA?
Which?	¿Cuál?	kwall?
Which one?	¿Cuál es?	kwall es?
Who?	¿Quién?	kyen?
whole	entero	enTEHro
Whose?	¿De quién?	deh kyen?
Why?	¿Por qué?	por kay?
Why not?	¿Cómo no?	COmo no?
wide	ancho	AHNcho
wind	viento	veeENtoh

English	Spanish	Pronunciation
window	la ventana	venTAna
-blind	celosía	selloSEEa
-frame	marco	MARco
-pane	cristal	creeSTALL
-screen	biombo	beeOHMbo
-sill	repisa	rehPEEsa
wire	alambre	ahLAHMbray
-brush	brocha	BROcha
wire mesh	tela metállica	TEla meTALeeca
wire strippers	pelacables	pelaCAbless
with	con	cohn
without	sin	seen
wood	la madera	la maDEHra
word	palabra	paLAbra
work	trabajo	traBAho
work, to	trabajar	trabaHAR
worker	trabajador	trabahaDOR
-compensation insurance	seguro de re embolsa	seGOOro deh reh emBOWLsa
wrench	llave	YAYvay
write, to	escribir	escreeBEER
Write it.	Escríbalo.	essCREEbalo.
yard	la yarda	YARda
square yard	cuadrada	kwaDRAda
year	año	AHNyo
yes	sí	see
yesterday	ayer	aYAIR
you (familiar)	tú	too
you (formal)	usted	ooSTED
you (plural)	ustedes	ooSTEDess
You must...	Debe...	DEHbeh...
your	su	soo
You're hired.	Usted está empleado.	ooSTED esTA emplehAHdoh
You're welcome.	De nada.	deh NAda
zip code	código postal	COdeego poSTAL
zoning permit	permiso en zonas	pairMEso en SOnahs

DICCIONARIO (Dictionary p. 56)

a plomo	plumb	plom
a través	across	aCROS
a través de	through	zru
abajo	down	daun
abanico	fan	fan
abejas	bees	biis
abierto	open	OUpen
abonar	fertilize	FERtilais
abrazadera	clamp	clamp
abrir	open	O-pen
acabado	finish	FINich
acabar	finish	FINich
accesorio	fitting	FITing
aceite	oil	oil
acera	sidewalk	SAIDuak
acero	steel	stiil
accidente	accident	AKsident
acondicionador de aire	air conditioner	er conDIchoner
acostar	lay out	lei aut
acotillo	sledgehammer	sledch-JAMer
adelantar	forward	FORuard
adentro	inside	inSAID
adentro de	into the	inTU de
adhesivo	adhesive	adJIsiv
adjustable llave	adjustable wrench	aYOStabel rench
adjustar	adjust	aYOST
adiós	goodbye	gudbai
aflojar	loosen	LUusen
afuera	outside	autsaid
agarrar	grab	grab
angosta	narrow	NEIRou
agua	water	UAter
filtro	filter	FEELter
medidor	meter	MIter
potable	drinking	DRINKing

aguarrás	paint thinner	peint ZIner
aguja	needle	NIdel
aguilón	gable	GEIbel
ahora	now	nau
ahora no	not now	not nau
ahorrar	save	seiv
aislamiento	insulation	insuLEIchon
aislar	insulate	INsuleit
al lado de	next to	nekst tu
al punto	instantly	INstantli
alambre	wire	uaier
alarma	alarm	aLARM
albañil	mason	MEIson
alcantarilla	sewer	SUer
aleros	eaves	iivs
alfiler	pin	pin
alfombra	carpet	CARpet
algo	some	som
alguna cosa	something	SOMzing
algunas veces	sometimes	SOMtaims
alicates	pliers	PLAIers
de extensión	channel lock	CHANel lok
almacén	warehouse	UEIRjaus
almuerzo	lunch	lonch
alrededor	around	aRAUND
alto	high	jai
alto voltaje	high voltage	jai VOLteich
alzar	set up	set op
alzamiento	hoist	joist
allá / allí	there	der
ambos	both	bouz
amigo	friend	frend
amolador	grinder	GRAINder
amolar	grind	graind
ancho	wide	uaid
andamio	scaffold	SCAfold
andar	walk	ualk
ángulo	angle	EINgl
año	year	iir
anteojos	goggles	GAgls

antepecho	sill	sil
anteproyecto	blueprint	blu-print
antes	before	biFOR
anticipo	advance, an	adVANS
apagado	off	off
apagar	turn off	tern off
aparato	appliance	aPLAIens
apartadero	siding	SAIding
apilar	stack	stak
aplicación	application	apliQUEIchon
aplicar (solicitar)	apply	aPLAI
aprender	learn	lern
apretado	tight	tait
apretar	tighten	TAIten
apron	apron	EIpron
aquí	here	jiir
arandela	washer	UAcher
árbol	tree	trii
arcos	arches	ARches
área	area	Eria
arena	sand	sand
arquitecto	architect	ARquitect
armadura	truss	tros
armario	closet	CLOset
armazón	frame	freim
arneses	harness	JARnes
arreglar	fix	fiks
arriba	up	op
artículo	fixture	FIXchur
asegura	fastener	FASner
asegurar	secure	sekiur
Así.	Like this.	laik dis.
asfálta	felt (techo)	felt
asfalto	asphalt	ASfalt
asiento	seat	siit
asistente	assistant	aSIStant
áspera	rough	roof
aspersor	sprinkler	SPRINkler
aspiradora	vacuum cleaner	VAcu-um CLIIner
atar	tie	tai

ático	attic	Atik
a tiempo	on time	on taim
atorarse	clogged	clogd
atornillar	screw	scruu
atrás	back	bak
a través	across	aCROS
ayer	yesterday	IESterdei
Ayúdalo.	Help him.	jelp jim.
Ayúdame.	Help me.	jelp mi.
ayudar	help	jelp
azadón	hoe	jou
azadonar	hoe	jou
azulejar	tile	tail
azulejo	tile (ceramic)	tail (ceRAMic)
bajar	lower	LOUr
bajo	down, low	daun, lou
más bajo	lower	LOUer
balcón	balcony	balCOUN
baldosa	tile (floor)	tail (flor)
banco	bench, bank	bench, bank
banda	strap	strap
baño	bathroom	BAZrum
bañera	bathtub	BAZtob
baranda	rail	reil
barato	cheap	chiip
barillas	re-bar	rii-bar
barra	bar, pry-bar	prai-bar
barrer	sweep	suiip
barrena	auger	AUger
barricada	barricade	BEIRikeid
base	base	beis
base de pintura	primer	PRAImer
bastante	enough	iNOF
basura	garbage	GARbich
bolsa	bag	bak
bote	can	kan
basurero	dumpster	DOMPster
batería	battery	BAteri
bienvenidos	welcome	UELcom

billete	bill	bil
biombo	screen	scriin
bisagra	hinge	jinch
blando	soft	soft
bloque	block	blok
bolsa	bag	bag
plásticas	plastic	PLAStik
bolsillo	pocket	POket
bomba	pump	pomp
bombilla	lightbulb	LAITboulb
boquilla	nozzle	NOSel
borde	border	BORder
bordillo	curb	curb
botas	boots	buuts
bote de basura	trash can	TRACHcan
brazo	bracket	BRAket
brea	tar	tar
brocha	brush	broch
bueno	good	gud
burletes	stripping	STRIPing
burro (para sierra)	saw horse	SAU jorss
buscador (poste)	stud finder	stad FAINder
Buscar...	Look for...	luk for...
buzón	mailbox	MEILboks
cabeza	head	jed
cabezal	header	JEDer
cable	cable	CEIbl
cabrio	rafter	RAFtr
cacerola	pan	pan
cada	each, every	iich, Evri
cadena	chain	chein
caer	fall	fol
café	coffee	COfi
caja	box	boks
de ingletes	miter box	MAIter boks
herramientas	tool box	tuul boks
cal	lime	laim
caladora	edger	EDcher
calafete	caulk	kok
pistola	gun	gon

calafetear	caulk	kok
calefacción	heating	JIting
calentador	heater	JIter
calentar	heat	jiit
calibre	gauge	geich
caliente	hot	jot
calmar	calm down	calm daun
calor	heat	jiit
calle	street	striit
callejón	alley	ALii
cama	bed	bed
cambiar	change	cheinch
cambio	change	cheinch
camino	road	roud
camión	truck	trok
camionero	truck driver	trok DRAIver
canelón	gutter	GOTter
canelón vertical	downspout	daun-spaut
cansado	tired	taird
caoba	mahogany	maJOGani
capataz	foreman	FORman
cargador	charger	CHARcher
cargar	load	loud
caro	expensive	eksPENsiv
carpintero	carpenter	CARpenter
carretilla	wheel barrow	JUIL BARou
carro	car, cart	car, cart
carro de mano	hand truck	jand trok
cartabón	bevel	BEvl
cartón	cardboard	CARDbord
casa	house	jaus
casco	helmet	JELmet
casi	almost	almoust
cedro	cedar	SIIdar
celosías	blinds	blainds
cemento	cement	siMENT
centavos	cents	cents
centro	center	SENter
cepillo	plane	plein
cera	wax	uaks

Spanish	English	Pronunciation
cerca	fence	fens
cerca de	near	niir
cerradura	lock	lok
cerrar	shut, lock	chot, lok
cerrucho	hand saw	jand sau
césped	lawn	lon
chapa	veneer	viNIIR
cierre	latch	latch
cinta	tape	teip
enmasca	masking	MASKin
metro	measure	MEchur
cinturón	belt	belt
cita	appointment	aPOINTment
claro	clear	clir
clavadora	nail gun	neil gon
clavar	nail	neil
clavija	dowel	dauel
clavos	nails	neils
cliente	client	CLAIent
clínica	clinic	CLInic
cobertizo	shed	ched
cobre	copper	COper
cocina	kitchen	KITchen
código postal	zip code	sip coud
colgante	hanger	JANGer
colgar	hang	jang
color	color	COLor
columna	column	COLom
combustible	fuel	fiul
comedor	dining room	DAIning rum
¿Cómo?	How?	jau?
¿Cómo no?	Why not?	juai not?
completar	complete	comPLIT
componente	component	comPOUnent
comprar	buy	bai
comprender	understand	onderSTAND
compressor	compressor	comPRESor
compuesto	compound	COMpaund
computadora	computer	comPIUter

con	with	uiz
concreto	concrete	CONcriit
bloque	block	blok
mezcla	mix	miks
conducir	drive	draiv
conducto	conduit	CONduit
conducto de aire	air duct	eir doct
conectar	connect	coNECT
conector	connector	coNECtor
congelando	freezing	FRIIsing
conseguir	get	get
Consiga...	Get...	get...
construcción	construction	conSTROKchon
construir	build	bild
contar	count	caunt
continuar	continue	conTINiu
contraventanas	shutters	CHOTers
contratista	contractor	CONtraktor
correcto	correct	coREKT
cortacésped	lawn mower	lon mouer
cortacircuitos	breaker	BREIkr
cortador	cutter	COTter
cortar	cut	cot
corto	short	chort
cosa	thing	zing
costa	cost	cost
crédito	credit	CREdit
cresta	ridge	ridch
cristal	pane	pein
cuadrado	square	sku-eir
cuadral	angle brace	EINgel breis
¿Cuál?	Which?	juich?
¿Cuál es?	Which one?	juich uan?
¿Cuándo?	When?	juen?
¿Cuánto?	How much?	jau moch?
¿Cuántos?	How many?	jau MEni?
cuarto	room, 1/4	ruum, uan KORter
cubo	bucket	BOket

Spanish	English	Pronunciation
cubierta	deck, casing	dek, KEIsing
cubrir	cover	COver
cuchillo	knife	naif
utilitario	utility	iuTILiti
cuenta	bill	bil
cuerda	cord	cord
Cuesta...	It costs...	it cost...
¡Cuidado!	¡Careful!	KEIRful!
cuña	wedge	uedch
cheque	check, bill	chek, bil
chimenea	fireplace	FAIrpleis
chófer	driver	DRAIver
dañado	damaged	DAMich
dar	give	guiv
de	from	from
De nada.	You're welcome.	ior UELcom
¿De quién?	Whose?	juus?
Debe...	You must...	iu most...
debajo	under	ONder
debajo de	below	bilou
decidir	decide	diSAID
decir	tell, say	tel, sei
dedo	finger	FINger
dejar	drop	drop
deletrear	spell	spel
delgado	thin	zin
¡Demasiado!	Too much!	tu moch!
Déme...	Give me...	guiv mi...
demora	delay	diLEI
dentro	into	intu
dentro de	insaid	insaid
depósito	storage	STORech
derecha	right	rait
derecho	straight	streit
derramarse	overflow	OUver-flou
Derribar.	Knock down.	nok daun.
desagüe	drain	drein

Spanish	English	Pronunciation
desatar	untie	anTAI
descansar	rest	rest
descargar	unload	anLOUD
desconectar	disconnect	discoNEKT
descubrir	uncover	onCOver
desenrollar	unroll	onROUL
¡Dése prisa!	Hurry up!	JURi op!
deshacer	undo	ondu
desigual	uneven	onIven
deslizar	slide	slaid
perno	bolt	bolt
puerta	door	dor
desmontar	dissassemble	disaSEMbl
desnudo	bare	beir
despacio	slowly	SLOUli
despejar	clear	cliir
desperdicios	scrap	scrap
después	later / after	LEItr / AFter
destornillador	screw driver	scru draiver
cruz:	phillips	FILips
plano	flat head	flat jed
detalle	detail	DIteil
detrás de	behind	biJAIND
devolver	return	riTERN
día	day	dei
día de pago	pay day	pei dei
día libre	day off	dei off
diagonales	diagonal	daiAGonal
diferente	different	DIFerent
difícil	difficult	DIFicolt
Dígame.	Tell me.	tel mi
dinero	money	MOni
dirección	address	ADdres
dirección electrónica	Email	II-meil
disco de arena	sanding disc	SANdin disk
diseño	design	deSAIN
diseñar	design	deSAIN
doblar	bend	bend

doctor	doctor	DOCtor
dólares	dollar	DOlar
¿Dónde?	Where?	juer?
¿Dónde está?	Where is?	juer is?
dos pisos	two story	tu STORi
dos por cuatro	two by four	tu bai for
dos por sies	two by six	tu bai siks
dos veces	twice	tuais
drenaje	drain	drein
ducha	shower	CHAUer
dueño	owner	OUner
duro	hard	jard
ebanista	cabinet maker	CABinet MEIker
edificio	building	BILding
código	code	coud
inpector	inspector	inSPECtor
permiso	permit	PERmit
efectivo	cash	kach
el	the / he / him	de / ji / jim
eléctrico	electric	iLECtric
extensión	cord	cord
electrista	electrician	ilecTRIchin
ella	her	jer
ellos	they	dei
embudo	funnel	FONel
emergencia	emergency	eMERgenci
empanelado	paneling	PANeling
empapelado	wallpaper	UALpeipcr
empaque	gasket	GASket
emparchar	patch (to)	patch (tu)
emparejar	match	match
empezar	start	start
empleado	employee	emploiII
emplear	employ	emploi
empujar	push	puch
en (gen)	in	in
(sobre)	on	on
en frente de	in front of	in front of

encender	turn on	tern on
encintar	tape	teip
enchufe	plug	plog
enchufes	outlets	AUTlets
encima	over / above	Over/aBOV
encontrar	find, meet	faind, meet
enfermo	sick	sik
enmarcar	frame	freim
enrejado	trellis	TRELis
enrollar	roll up	roul op
entablado	flooring	FLORing
entender	understand	onderSTAND
entero	whole	joul
entonces	then	den
entrada	entrance	ENtrans
entrar	enter	ENter
entre	between	biTUIIN
equipo	equipment	iQUIPment
es	is	is
escado (cara)	face shield	feis chiild
escalera	ladder	LADer
escaleras	stairs	steirs
escalón	step	step
escoba	broom	bruum
Escribalo.	Write it.	rait it.
escriba	write	rait
escuadra	square	skueir
¡Escuche!	Listen!	LISen!
ese/esos	that / those	dat / dous
eso es todo	that's all	dats ol
esparcir	spread	spred
espejo	mirror	MIRor
¡Espere!	Wait!	ueit!
esponja	sponge	sponch
espuma	foam	foum
estaca	stake	steik
estacionar	park	park
Estados Unidos	United States	iuNAIted steits
estándar	standard	STANdard

Spanish	English	Pronunciation
estaño	tin	tin
estatales	state	steit
éste	this	dis
estiércol	manure	manuur
estimación	estimate	EStimeit
esto / estos	this / these	dis/diis
Esto funciona.	It works.	it uerks.
estuco	stucco	STOco
estudio	den	den
Excava	Dig	dig
excusado	toilet	TOIlet
expansión	expansion	eksPANchon
explicar	explain	eksPLEIN
extensión	extension cord	eksTENchon cord
exterior	exterior	exTIRior
extintor	fire extinguisher	FAIer ekSTINgüicher
fachada	facade	faSAD
fácil	easy	Isi
factura	invoice	INvois
faja	fascia	FEIsia
fecha	date	deit
felpa	roof felt	ruf felt
ferretería	hardware	JARDueir
fin	end, tip	end, tip
fino (veta)	fine	fain
final	final	FAInal
firmar	sign	sain
flotador	float	flout
flores	flowers	FLAUers
fondo	bottom	BOtom
formón	chisel	CHIsel
formones	gouges	GAUches
formulario	form	form
fósforos	matches	MATCHes
frágil	fragil	FRAchel
frente	front	front

frío	cold	cold
fruta	fruit	frut
fuego	fire	FAIr
fuente	fountain	FAunten
fuera	out	aut
fuerte	strong	strong
fumar	smoking	SMOUkin
fundación	foundation	faunDEIchon
fusible	fuse	fius
gabinete	cabinet	CABinet
galón	gallon	GALon
gancho	hook	juk
garaje	garage	gaRACH
garantía	guarantee	garanTI
gas	gas	gas
gasolina	gasoline	GASolin
gato	jack	chak
gato		
(estante de)	jack stands	chak stans
gaveta	drawer	drour
generador	generator	GENereitor
giro postal	money order	MOni ORder
goma	glue	glu
golpear	hit	jit
gota	drop	drop
gotear	dripping	DRIPing
gracias	thanks	zanks
grado	degree, grade	deGR, greid
grande	large	larch
granito	granite	GRAnit
grapa	clamp	clamp
grapa de C	C-clamp	SI-clamp
grapadora	stapler	STEIpler
grapas	staples	STEIpls
pistola	gun	gon
grapón	brace	breis
grasa	grease	griis
grava	gravel	GROvel

grieta	**crack**	crak
guantes	**gloves**	glovs
Guarda...	**Put away...**	put aUEI...
guardar	**keep**	kiip
Guárdelo.	**Keep it.**	kiip it.
hablar	**speak**	spiik
hacer (gen)	**make**	meik
(ejecutar)	**do**	du
hacha	**axe**	aks
Hágalo.	**Do it.**	du it.
hambre	**hungry**	JONgri
Hay...	**There is...**	der is...
herido	**hurt**	jurt
herramienta	**tool**	tuul
caja	box	boks
eléctrica	power	PAUer
hoja (taladro)	**bit**	bit
hoja (sierra)	**blade**	bleid
hoja (plano)	**sheet**	chiit
hojas (arbol)	**leaves**	liivs
hoyo	**hole**	joul
hombre	**man**	man
hondo	**deep**	dip
hora	**hour**	AUer
horario	**schedule**	SKEdiul
horizontal	**horizontal**	joriZONtal
hormigas	**ants**	ants
hospital	**hospital**	JOSpital
hoy	**today**	tuDEI
hueco	**socket**	SOKet
identificación	**identification**	aidentifiQUEchon
imán	**magnet**	MAGnet
importante	**important**	imPORtant
impuestos	**taxes**	taxes
formulario	form	form
federales	federal	FEDeral
estatales	state	steit

incorporado	built-in	BILT-in
incorrecto	incorrecto	incorRECT
indicador	indicator	INdicater
indicar	point to	point tu
ingeniero	engineer	en-llin-IIR
inglete	miter	MAIter
insecticida	insecticide	inSECtisaid
insecto	insect	INsect
inspector	inspector	inSPECtor
instalar	install	inSTOL
instrucción	instruction	inSTROCchon
interruptor	switch	suich
interior	interior	inTERior
interpretar	interpret	inTERpret
inverso	reverse	riVERS
ir	go	gou
izquierda	left	left
jabón	soap	soup
jalar	pull	pul
jamba	jamb	cham
jardín	garden	GARden
jardinero	gardener	GARdener
jefe	boss	bos
jergón	pallet	PALet
juntar	assemble	aSEMbl
junto a	beside	biSAID
juntos	together	tuGUEder
la, las, los	the	de
laca	lacquer	LAker
lado	side	said
ladrillo	brick	brik
ladrillero	bricklayer	BRIKlei-er
lamento (queja)	complaint	comPLEINT
lámpara	lamp	lamp
lápiz	pencil	PENcil
largo	long	long

lata	can	can
lata	tin	tin
tijeras	snips	snips
latón	brass	brass
lavadero	sink	sink
lavar	wash	uach
lazo	tie	tai
lazo abajo	tie downs	tai dauns
lechada	grout	graut
leer	read	riid
lento	slow	slou
lesión	injury	inlluri
levantar	lift	lift
libra (s)	pound (s)	paund (s)
licencia	license	LAIsens
de conducir	drivers license	DRAIvers LAIsens
ligero	light	lait
lijar	sand	sand
lijadora	sander	SANDer
lima	file	fail
limar	file	fail
limpiar	clean, to	cliin
linea	line	lain
linóleo	linoeum	liNOlium
linterna	flashlight	FLACHlait
lista	list	list
listo	ready	REdi
lo	it	it
lodo	mud	mod
Lo siento.	I'm sorry.	aim SOri
lona	tarp	tarp
los	the, them	de, dem
losa	slab	slab
luz	light	lait
llamar	call	col
llave (cerrar)	key	ki
(lavabo)	faucet	FOset
(heramnta)	wrench	rench
llave de hueco	socket wrench	SOKet rench

Spanish	English	Pronunciation
llave de tubo	pipe wrench	paip rench
llaves tornos	vice grips	vais grips
llenar	fill	fil
lleno	full	ful
llevar (ropa)	wear	uer
(carga)	carry	KEIRri
lluvia	rain	rein
maceta	planter	PLANter
madera	lumber	LOMber
laminada	plywood	PLAIuod
o dura	hardwood	JARDuod
malgastar	waste	ueist
malo	bad	bad
mañana (alba)	morning	MORnin
mañana	tomorrow	tuMOrou
mandar	send	send
mandos	controls	conTROLS
mandril	chuck	chok
manga	sliiv	sliiv
mango	handle	JANdl
manguera	hose	jous
mano	hand	jand
manta	blanket	BLANket
mantener	maintain	meintein
mañana	morning	MORning
mango	handle	JANdel
mantener	maintain	meintein
máquina	machine	maCHIIN
mancha	stain	stein
mapa	map	map
marcar	mark	mark
mármol	marble	MARbel
martillo	hammer	JAmer
más	more	mor
más pequeño	smaller	smoler
más tarde	later	LEIter
máscara	mask	mask

masilla	putty	POti
espátula	knife	naif
masonita	masonite	MEIsonait
mástique	mastic	MAStic
material	material	maTIRial
mazo	mallet	MALet
me	me	mi
Me gusta...	I like...	ai laik...
mécanico	mechanic	meCANic
medicina	medicine	MEDicin
medidor	meter	MIter
medio	middle	MIDel
mediodía	noon	nuun
medir	measure	MEchur
mejor	better	BEter
menos	less	less
mensaje	message	MESich
ménsula	bracket	BRAket
mercado	market	MARket
mes	month	monz
mesa	table	TEIbul
metal	metal	METal
hoja	sheet	chiit
mezcladora	mixer	MIKSer
mezclar	mix	miks
mi	my	mai
Mídelo.	Measure it.	MEchur it.
mil	thousand	ZAUsand
milla	mile	mail
mio	mine	main
minuto	minute	MInut
mira	look	luk
mirar	watch	uatch
mismo	same	seim
milla	mile	mail
moho	mold	mold
mojado	wet	uet
molde	form	form
moldura	molding	MOLdin

moneda	coin	coin
montante	stud	stad
montura	saddle	SADel
mortero	mortar	MORtur
mostrador	counter	CAUNter
mostrar	show	CAUNter
mover	move	muv
mucho	much	moch
muchos	many	MEni
muebles	furniture	FURnechur
muerto perno	dead bolt	ded bolt
muescar	notch	notch
Muéstreme.	Show me.	chou mi.
mueve	move	muuv
muy	very	VEri
nada	nothing	NOzin
nadie	nobody	NObadi
necesitar	need	niid
¿Necesitas?	Do you need?	du iu nid?
Necesito...	I need...	ai niid...
nombre	name	neim
ninguno	none	non
nivel (heramnta)	level	LEvel
nivelar	level	LEvel
no...	no, don't...	no, dount...
No entre.	Keep out.	kiip aut.
No fumar.	No smoking.	no SMOUkin.
No puedo...	I can't...	ai cant...
No sirve.	Out of order.`	aut af ORder.
No use.	Don't use.	dount ius.
noche	night	nait
nombre	name	neim
nosotros	we, us	ui, os
nuevo	new	niu
número	number	NOMber
nunca	never	NEver

o	or	or
obrero	worker	uerker
ocupado	busy	BIsi
oferta	bid	bid
oficina	office	OFis
ojos	eyes	aiss
protección	protection	proTECchon
operar	operate	OPereit
opuesto	opposite	OPousit
orden	order	ORder
de compra	purchase order	PURches ORder
ordenar	order	ORder
oscuro	dark	dark
otra vez	again	aGEIN
otro	other	Oder
otro lado	other side	Oder said
paga	pay	pei
pagar	pay	pei
paisaje	landscape	LANDskcip
paisajero	landscaper	LANDskeiper
pala	shovel	CHOvel
palear	shovel	CHOvel
palabra	word	uerd
palada	shovelfull	CHOvelful
palanca	lever	LEver
paleta	trowel	TRAUel
palo	stick	stik
panel	panel	PANel
papel	paper	PEIper
papel de brea	tar paper	tar PEIper
papel de lija	sand paper	sand PEIper
para	for	for
Para a las...	Stop at...	stop at...
parapeto	parapet	PEIRapet
parcela	lot	lot
parche	patch	patch
parchar	patch	patch
¡Pare!	Stop!	stop!

pared	wall	ual
parte	part	part
partir	leave	liiv
pasillo	hall	jal
patio	patio	PAtio
pavimento	pavement	PEIVment
pedazo	piece	piis
pedir	ask	ask
pega	glue	glu
pegar	glue	glu
pelacables	wire strippers	uair STRIPpers
peligroso	dangerous	DEINlleros
pensar	think	zink
pequeño	small	smol
perdido	lost	lost
perdón	excuse me	exKIUS mi
perforadora	jack hammer	chak JAMer
permiso	permit	PERmit
perno	bolt	bolt
pernos		
de anclaje	anchor bolt	ANkor bolt
de palanca	toggle bolt	TOgel bolt
perro	dog	dog
pesado	heavy	JEvi
peso (libra)	weight	ueit
pico (heramnta)	pick	pik
pide	ask	ask
pie	foot	fut
cuadrado	square	skiuer
piedra	stone	stoun
pila (montón)	pile	pail
pinta (medida)	pint	paint
pintar	paint	peint
pintura	paint	peint
pinza	clip	clip
piscina	pool	puul
piso	floor	flor
pistola	gun	gon
plan de suelo	floor plan	flor plan
plano	even, flat	Iven, flat

110

planos	plans	plans
plantar	plant	plant
plantas	plants	plants
plantilla	jig	chig
plástico	plastic	PLAStic
plato	plate	pleit
a plomo	plumb	plom
plomada	plumb	plom
plomería	plumbing	PLOmin
plomero	plumber	PLOmer
pluma	pen	pen
poco	little	LITel
poder	can	can
podar	prune	pruun
polvo	powder	PAUder
pomo	knob	nob
poner	put	put
ponerse	put on	put on
Póngalo...	Put it...	put it...
polvo	dust	dost
máscara	mask	mask
por	for	for
por favor	please	pliis
¿Por qué?	Why?	juai?
porche	porch	porch
porque	because	biCOS
portal (pórtico)	porch	porch
(entrada)	hall	jal
portátil	portable	PORtabel
portón	gate	geit
poste	post	post
practicar	practice	PRACtis
precio	price	preis
preguntar	question	CUESchon
preparar	prepare	priPEIR
presión	pressure	PREchur
lavar	wash	uach
primer piso	first floor	first flor

primeros auxilios	first aid	furst eid
principal	main	mein
Privado.	Private.	PRAIvet.
probar	test	test
problema	problem	PROblem
pronto	quickly	KUIKli
pronunciar	pronounce	proNAUNS
propiedad	property	PROperti
protección	protection	prouTEKchon
proteger	protect	prouTEKT
próximo	next	nekst
proyección	overhang	OUver-jang
proyecto	project	PROchect
prueba	test	test
¿Puede?	Can you...?	can iu...?
Puedo	I Can...	ai can...
¿Puedo?	Can I...?	¿can ai...?
puerta	door	dor
pulir	polish	PAUlich
punzones	punches	PANCHes
pulgada(s)	inch(es)	INch(es)
pulir	polish	POLich
punta	tip, point	tip, point
punta de cruz	phillips head	FIlips jed
punzones	punches	PONCHes

¿Qué?	What?	juat?
¿Qué es esto?	What's this?	juats dis?
¿Qué hora?	What time?	juat taim?
quedar	stay	stei
quemar	burn	bern
querer	want	uant
querosén	kerosene	KEIRosin
¿Quien?	Who?	ju?
quitar	remove	riMUV
quizás	maybe	MEIbi

radio	radio	REIdio
raíz	root	ruut
rama	branch	branch
rampa	ramp	ramp
ramura	groove	gruuv
rápido	fast	fast
rascador	scraper	SCREIper
raspar	scrape	screip
rastrillar	rake	reik
rastrillo	rake	reik
recámara	bedroom	BEDrum
recibo	receipt	riSIIT
recientemente	recently	RIcentli
recipiente	container	conTEIner
recoger	pick up	pik op
recortar	trim	trim
recto de angulo	right angle	rait ANgel
reemplazar	replace	riPLEIS
referencia	referral	riFERel
refrigerador	refrigerator	riFRICHereitor
refuerzo	reinforced	ri-enFORST
regar	water	UAter
regla	straightedge	streit-ech
regla T	T square	TI skuier
regresar	go back	gou bak
rejilla de aire	air vent	eir vent
remolque	trailer	TREIler
reparador	repairman	riPEIR-man
reparar	repair	riPEIR
¡Repita!	Repeat!	riPIIT!
respalda	backing	BAKin
respiradero	vent	vent
respirador	respirator	RESpireitor
reverso	reverse	RIvers
revisar	check	chek
rincón	corner	CORner
ripia	shingle	CHINgel
roble	oak	ouk
rocas	rocks	roks
rociador	sprinkler	SPRINKler

rociadora	sprayer	SPREIer
rociar	spray	sprei
pistola	gun	gon
rodillo	roller	ROler
romper	break	breik
ropero	closet	CLOset
roto	broken	BROUken
saber	know	nou
sacaclavos	nail puller	neil PULer
sacar	take away	teik auei
sala	livingroom	LIVing-ruum
salida	exit	EXit
salir	exit	EXit
¿Se puede?	May I...?	mei ai...?
secar	dry	drai
sección	section	SECchon
seco	dry	drai
sed	thirsty	ZURSti
seguir	follow	FAlou
segundo	second	SECond
seguridad	safety	SEIFti
vidrio	glass	glas
gafas	glasses	GLASes
arneses	harness	JARness
línea	line	lain
seguridad	safety	SEIFti
pasamanos	rails	reils
seguro social	social security	SOUchol seCIURiti
tarjeta	card	(card)
seguros	insurance	inCHURans
de re embolsa	compensation	compenSEIchon
responsabilidad	liability	lai-aBILiti
sellante	sealant	SIILant
sellar	seal	siil
semana	week	uik
sembrar	plant, seed	plant, siid
señalar	point (to)	point (tu)
señales	signs, signals	sains, signals

señor	sir	sur
señora	Mrs./Ma'am	MISes/mam
sensor de humo	smoke detector	smouk diTECtor
separación	partition	parTIchon
separar	separate	SEPereit
séptico	septic	SEPtic
ser	is	is
serrucho	saw	so
servicio	service panel	SERvis PAnel
si	yes	ies
sierra	saw	sau
hoja	blade	bleid
sierra de		
cadena	chain saw	chein so
fija	radial	REIdial
mesa	table	TEIbel
recíproco	reciprocating	riCIProukeitin
circular	circular	CIRcular
disco	blade	-bleid
sierra para		
metales	hack saw	JOC-so
sifón	trap	trap
Sígame.	Follow me.	FAlou mi.
silla	chair	cheir
similar	similar	SIMilar
sin	without	uizAUT
sindicato	union	IUNion
sitio (trabajo)	job site	chob sait
sobre	on top of	on top of
¡Soccoro!	Help!	¡jelp!
sofito	soffit	SAfit
soga	rope	roup
sol	sun	son
soldador	solderer	SAderer
soldadura	solder	ueld
soldar	weld	ueld
solamente	only	OUNli
solicitud	application	apliQUEIchon
sólido	solid	SOlid

Spanish	English	Pronunciation
soltar	loosen	LUsen
sopapa	plunger	PLONller
soplador	blower	BLOUer
soporte	support	suPORT
soportar	support	suPORT
sostener	hold	jould
sótano	basement	BEISment
Soy...	I'm...	aim...
su	your	ior
subcontratista	subcontractor	sabcontractor
sube	get up	get op
subir	climb	claim
subterráneo	underground	ondergraund
sucio	dirty	DURti
suelo	ground	graund
suelto	loose	luss
suficiente	enough	iNOF
sujetar	attach	aTACH
sumar	add	ad
superficie	surface	SERfeis
tabla	board	bourd
de partícula	particle	PARtikel
tachón	stud	stod
tachuela	tack	tak
taladrar	drill	dril
taladro	drill	dril
tamaño	size	sais
tanque	tank	tank
tapa	lid, top	lid, top
tapajuntas	flashing	FLACHin
tapónes de oído	ear plugs	ir plags
tarde	afternoon	AFternuun
tardío	late	leit
tarjeta	card	card
verde	green	griin
taza	cup	cop
techero	roofer	RUUFer

116

techo (exterior)	**roof**	ruuf
(dentro)	**ceiling**	SIIling
teja	**tile** (roof)	tail (ruf)
tela metállica	**wire mesh**	uair mech
teléfono	**telephone**	telefoun
temperatura	**temperature**	TEMPeratur
temprano	**early**	ERli
tener	**have**	jav
Tengo...	**I have...**	ai jav...
terminar	**finish, fire**	FInich
termitas	**termites**	TERmaits
terraza	**deck**	dek
terrazo	**ceramic tile**	serAMic tail
tiempo (lluvia..)	**weather**	UEder
tiempo (hora)	**time**	taim
hoja	**sheet**	chiit
tienda	**store**	stor
¿Tiene...?	**Are you...?**	ar iu...?
¿Tienes?	**Do you have?**	du iu jav?
tierra	**dirt**	durt
tijeras	**scissors**	SIsors
grande	**clippers**	CLIpers
metal	**tin snips**	tin snips
timbre	**door bell**	dor bel
tintura	**stain**	stein
tirante	**brace**	breis
tirar	**throw away**	zrou aUEI
tiza	**chalk**	chok
tocar	**touch**	toch
tocón	**stump**	stomp
todo	**all**	ol
todo el mundo	**everybody**	EVribodi
toldo	**awning**	AUning
tomar	**take, drink**	teik, drink
tope	**top**	top
torcer	**twist**	tuist
tornillo	**screw**	scruu
pistola	**gun**	gon
torno de banco	**vise**	vais
trabajar	**work**	uerk

trabajo	work, job	uerk, chob
trabajador	worker	UERKer
Traduce.	Translate.	TRANSleit
traductor	interpreter	inTERpreter
traer	bring	bring
tragaluz	skylight	SKAIlait
Tráigame...	Bring me...	bring mi...
transportacción	transportation	transporTEIchon
trapeador	mop	mop
trapo	cloth, rag	cloz, rag
traslapo	overlap	OUver-lap
tratar	try	trai
trinquete	ratchet	RATchet
troca (camión)	truck	trok
tu	you	iu
tubería	plumbing	PLOMin
tubo	pipe	paip
tuerca	nut	not

último	last	last
umbral	threshold	TRECHjould
un	a	ei
un pedazo	a piece	a piis
un poco	a little	a LItel
una cosa	a thing	a zing
un momento	one moment	uan MOUment
una vez	once	uans
unidad	unit	IUnit
uniforme	uniform	IUniform
unión	joint	choint
la macilla	compound	COMpaund
uno por cuatro	one by four	uan bai for
usar	use	ius
usted	you	iu
ustedes	you all	iu all
utilidades	utilities	iuTILitis
va	go	gou
vacío	empty	EMti
vaciar	empty	EMti

118

válvula	valve	valv
Vámonos.	Let's go.	lets gou.
vara	rod	rod
varillas	re-bar	rii-bar
¡Váya!	go!	gou!
Váya con el.	Go with him.	gou uiz jim.
valle	valley	VALi
vegetale	vegetable	VECHtabel
vehículo	vehicle	VI-jicol
¡Ven acá!	Come here!	com jier!
venda	bandage	BANdich
veneno	poison	POIson
venir	come	com
ventana	window	UINdou
biombo	screen	skriin
celosía	blind	blaind
cristal	pane	pein
marco	frame	freim
repisa	sill	sil
ventilar	ventilate	VENtileit
ventilador	fan	fan
ver	see	sii
vertical	vertical	VERtical
veta	grain	grein
vid	vine	vain
vidriero	glazier	GLEIziir
vidrio	glass	glas
templado	tempered	TEMperd
viejo	old	ould
viento	wind	uind
viga	beam	biim
vigueta	joist	choist
vinilo	vinyl	VAInel
voltio	volt	volt
110	one ten	uan ten
220	two twenty	tu tuen-ti
voltear	turn	turn
volúmen	volume	VOLium

y	**and**	and
yarda	**yard**	iard
cuadrada	**square**	skueir
yerbajos	**weeds**	uiids
yeso	**plaster**	PLASter
(panel)	**drywall**	DRAIual
Yo	**I**	ai
Yo cobro...	**I charge...**	ai charch...
Yo necesito...	**I need...**	ai niid...
Yo quiero...	**I want...**	ai uant...
Yo sé...	**I know...**	ai nou...
Yo soy...	**I am...**	ai am...
Yo voy...	**I'm going...**	aimGOUing...
zacate	**grass**	gras
zanja	**trench**	trench
	ditch	ditch
zócalo	**baseboard**	BEISbord

NOTAS

This book helps communication and learning, but is not always "textbook" English or Spanish.

Este libro ayuda en la comunicación y el aprendizaje, pero no representa siempre el inglés o español textual.

www.easyspanishforconstruction.com

Mitchell Brothers Press
Impresos Hermanos Mitchell